INTERNATIONAL NORMS AND MOBILIZATION OF DEMOCRACY

International Norms and Mobilization of Democracy
Nicaragua in the world

MANUEL OROZCO
Inter-American Dialogue

LONDON AND NEW YORK

First published 2002 by Ashgate Publishing

Reissued 2018 by Routledge
2 Park Square, Milton Park, Abingdon, Oxon OX14 4RN
711 Third Avenue, New York, NY 10017, USA

Routledge is an imprint of the Taylor & Francis Group, an informa business

Copyright © Manuel Orozco 2002

Manuel Orozco has asserted his moral right to be identified as the author of this work in accordance with the Copyright, Designs and Patents Act, 1988.

All rights reserved. No part of this book may be reprinted or reproduced or utilised in any form or by any electronic, mechanical, or other means, now known or hereafter invented, including photocopying and recording, or in any information storage or retrieval system, without permission in writing from the publishers.

Notice:
Product or corporate names may be trademarks or registered trademarks, and are used only for identification and explanation without intent to infringe.

Publisher's Note
The publisher has gone to great lengths to ensure the quality of this reprint but points out that some imperfections in the original copies may be apparent.

Disclaimer
The publisher has made every effort to trace copyright holders and welcomes correspondence from those they have been unable to contact.

A Library of Congress record exists under LC control number: 2002100328

ISBN 13: 978-1-138-74109-6 (hbk)
ISBN 13: 978-1-138-74108-9 (pbk)
ISBN 13: 978-1-315-18302-2 (ebk)

Contents

Figures and Tables   *vi*
Acknowledgment   *vii*

1   Introduction: International Relations, Norms and Democracy   1

2   International Dimension of Democracy: Trends and Dynamics   6

3   The Emergence of an International Norm for Democratization   29

4   The International Political Context of Nicaragua: from U.S. Intervention to International Involvement   52

5   Negotiating Peace and Holding Elections   66

6   Democratization in the Aftermath of Civil War: Nicaragua in the 1990s   91

7   Limitations of the International Mobilization for Democracy   109

Bibliography   *128*
Index   *146*

Figures and Tables

Figure 2.1 Democratization since 1950	6
Figure 2.2 Rise of International NGOs, 1956-1999	10
Table 2.1 Actors, Mechanisms and Conditions for Mobilization	28
Table 3.1 Wars by Region and Type, 1945-1994	42
Figure 3.1 Worldwide Elections and UN Assistance	50
Table 3.2 Global Conferences on Democracy	51
Table 4.1 Foreign Aid by Socialist Countries to Nicaragua, 1979-1989	54
Table 4.2 Official Development Assistance to Nicaragua, 1980-1989	55
Table 4.3 Democracy Assistance Programs by International Donors	58
Table 4.4 Assistance for Democracy by Sector	60
Table 4.5 Democratic Assistance by Sector and Region or Country	61
Table 4.6 International NGOs in Nicaragua: Distribution by Financial Contributions and Number of Organizations (1990-1996)	63
Table 5.1 Human and Economic Costs of the War	68
Table 5.2 Negotiations in Nicaragua: Main Agreements Reached	79
Table 5.3 U.S. Funding for the Nicaraguan Elections	85
Table 5.4 Issues Considered for Electoral Monitoring	87
Table 6.1 Civil Disobedience in Nicaragua, 1991-1995	93
Table 6.2 Founding Years of 239 NGOs in Nicaragua	96
Table 6.3 Number of Observers by People and Groups	99
Table 6.4 Size of Bureaucracy in Nicaragua	100
Figure 6.1 GDP Per Capita, 1988-1999	102
Table 6.5 International Actors in Nicaragua	104
Table 6.6 Major Political Events in Nicaragua in the 1990s	107
Table 7.1 Municipal Election: Votes by Party and Department	118
Figure 7.1 Decline of Arnoldo Alemán's Popularity	119
Table 7.2 Public Opinion Polls in Support of Presidential Candidates	120
Table 7.3 Nicaraguan Elections since 1990	121
Table 7.4 Observation Assistance to *Etica y Transparencia*	122

Acknowledgment

This book is an important reminder that choices and efforts are not only the product of individual decisions, but also of direct and indirect collective engagement. Both the experience of international support for democracy and this book itself are testament to such involvement.

When the Somoza regime was overthrown in 1979, Nicaraguans thanked the international community for their support to end a forty year dictatorship. This book validates the efforts of national and international actors advocating democracy. In particular, it recognizes the work of those who mobilized international attention to promote democratic change in countries like Nicaragua. Former president Oscar Arias is an example of advocacy to end war and extend democracy in Central America. And former president Violeta Chamorro represents an individual committed to democracy. In addition to her dedication to Nicaraguans, she sought the attention of the international community and their support to bring stability into her country. This book is dedicated to her.

Although it is customary to say that one's writings are solely one's own responsibility and that is true, credit is owed to those who facilitate our academic training, contribute to shaping our ideas and ideals about social and political change and who encourage our theoretical reflection. I identify only four of those people here, but thank the contributions of many others. From developing the idea itself to the delivery of the final product, I have received the guiding support of a number of people; friends, professors, relatives, acquaintances, and strangers. First and foremost, Fran Buntman, my wife and colleague, is the most influential person on this work. I thank her for her active support. She has seen the progress and results of my work and study of international norms and mobilization for democracy. In her commitment to justice and democracy she has validated and supported my own commitments. Another person who has been helpful to this project is my friend and colleague Mignone Vega, a democracy advocate who has seen the many facets and risks of democratization. I thank my former professors and colleagues, Rodolfo de la Garza and Pope Atkins whose trust and support have been present at all times. Finally, I thank Bruce Bueno de Mesquita who helped shape my political thinking. Although this book is not an expected utility analysis, it reflects his confidence in me and the lessons I learned from him many years ago.

Chapter 1

Introduction: International Relations, Norms and Democracy

For the first time ever, in 1989, an independent country, Nicaragua, agreed that the international community[1] supervise its national elections. This event represented a turning point in which the United Nations "broke its unblemished 'hands-off' record by sending an election team to Nicaragua" (Rosenau 1996, 264). The request and the response to it symbolized an emerging international consensus to protect and support democracy in individual nations. Moreover, the political context in which these elections were agreed upon was itself a product of international dedication to end civil war and promote democracy in the Central American region. Led by Costa Rica's president, Oscar Arias, and at the urging of the United Nations (UN) and the Organization of American States (OAS), in 1987 Central American leaders agreed to peace negotiations and free and fair elections, with Nicaragua starting the process of achieving peace and democracy simultaneously. Furthermore, these elections would be internationally monitored to guarantee unbiased results that reflected the will of the people.

The peace agreement that emerged from the 1987 talks and the Nicaraguan election in 1990 are emblematic of an international community concerned with introducing and consolidating democracy in Nicaragua and elsewhere, and with linking democratization to conflict resolution.

Unlike most democratic transitions that occurred in the 1980s, Nicaragua's transition was shaped by a civil war. The legacy of war constituted a major challenge as the prevailing culture of violence and polarization increased the difficulty of any effort to achieve national

---

[1] A useful definition of international community is offered by Kumar , "a general category to refer to multilateral and bilateral agencies, governments, intergovernmental organizations, international non-governmental organizations, philanthropic organizations, private sector firms"(Kumar 1997, 3). In speaking of international community, I also agree with Rosenau (1997, 180) that sometimes "reference is made with the United Nations in mind, but frequently it is voiced in the context of a less organized but no less specific actor...[that] is rather conceived to be an empirical reality, an actor that has obligations, responsibilities, and capabilities even if it lacks desirable structures."

reconciliation. After the installation of the new government under President Violeta Chamorro, however, the country embarked on a series of attempts to improve political conditions amid a climate of polarization and violence.

The 1990 election gave impetus to international support for the country's democratic transition. International actors provided critical support to rebuild political institutions, social capital, and national trust that had been decimated over years of dictatorship, revolution, and war. A wide number of international actors, ranging from countries like the United States, Sweden, and Costa Rica, to foundations and other international civil society groups, implicated themselves in democratizing Nicaragua by mediating conflicts, developing the civil society sector, and monitoring elections. Rather than having an intermittent participation, most of these actors aimed to create and build democratic institutions in order to provide roots for a new political culture.

International Norms

International involvement in democracy promotion around the world uses various incentives and mechanisms of influence to create political change. This activism reflects a normative commitment to democracy that evolves from notions of sovereignty and human rights. Norms, or shared understandings of standards for behavior, are the result of the interaction among social groups and their intention to conform to some social practice (Searle 1995). A key attribute of norms is their durability and clarity, as well as their capacity to be translated into law, or into a customary practice prescribing moral or social behavior (Arend 1999). Recent approaches concerning norms and ideas in international relations have improved our understandings of international interaction (Kubalkova 1998; Onuf 1998). They have shown that international norms have consequences and implications for international action.

In the case of democratization, emerging international norms for democracy promotion have contributed to provide the rationale for diverse external mobilization. This involvement has reflected the view that democracy and freedom in only one or one's own country is no longer sufficient to support democracy as a principle and a practice. As a result democracy promotion has gradually been adopted as a normative practice that arises out of the influence of previously existing institutions that foster democracy, the efforts of international advocates for democracy and human rights, and changing trends in the world.

Individuals, organizations, and states have endorsed and mobilized towards the global achievement and right of citizens to elect their governments, thus extending and deepening liberties and democratic rights across national borders. This book traces the ways in which external actors contributed significantly to bring democratic change to Nicaragua in the 1990s. It shows how political change towards democratization depended on diplomatic pressure, incentives, and democracy assistance programs intended to introduce and then support democratization.

Key Issues and Current Studies on Democracy

Three questions lie at the core of this work. What motivations, if any, do international actors have to support democratic change? Are international actors key players in building democracy? And can democracy succeed amid the legacy of a civil war? Although these questions are of fundamental relevance in today's world politics, there are very few studies that focus on democratic transitions after civil war, and on the role and motivations of international action in building democratic change. In looking at the Nicaraguan experience a theoretical building block can be established as to the relationship between democracy, post-conflict developments, and international relations.

The meaning of democracy has been debated in terms of both its procedures and outcomes. Some definitions stress the delivery of people's will as the core meaning of democracy, while others argue that democracy is the process by which rule by the people is guaranteed and effected. In the first case, the emphasis is on 'outcomes' or substance, delivery rather than institutions. Gills, Rocamora, and Wilson (1993, 5), for example, argue that 'formal' or institutional democracy "without social reform increases economic inequality and thereby intensifies unequal distribution of power in society. The most important task of democratic regimes is social reform. In the absence of progressive social reform the term 'democracy' is largely devoid of meaningful content." Robinson (1996, 218) takes this argument much further, claiming that what we conventionally know as 'Western democracy' is not democracy at all but "a political system corresponding to the capitalist mode of production and distinct from authoritarianism insofar as it rests on social control of subordinate groups through consensual mechanisms." This perspective, however, obscures or rejects people's capacity to exercise their rule in democratic institutions. Robinson and others understate or ignore the importance of formal equal rights and legal freedom.

At minimum, rule by the people requires procedural rights for citizens to choose their own government. Thus, there needs to be civil and political rights which in turn must be enforced and protected. Furthermore, notions of 'social reform' will, or should, emerge from the polity, but may not be "progressive" social reform if the citizenry is conservative or if the state imposes on the citizen's will, for example. In many societies, the average citizen holds rather conservative views about politics, society, and the economy. Democracies become meaningless when they do not follow social demands, which in turn are more complex than economic redistribution schemes. Thus, without an institutional framework, it is not possible to have a substantive democratic regime.

In the second case, scholars like Diamond and Dahl have stressed a process-based perspective of democracy. Diamond advocates a definition of democracy composed of four features: competition for power, inclusive political participation, guarantees of civil and political liberties, and accountability of rulers for their actions (Diamond 1996, 55). To Diamond, democracy is found at one extreme of the political spectrum, with authoritarianism on the other end. Larry Diamond also distinguishes two kinds of democracy that fall along this continuum. The first, electoral democracy, reflects a minimalist conception that is defined as "a regime in which governmental offices are filled as a consequence of contested elections" (Przeworski 1996, 50-51). The second conception, liberal democracy, demands freedoms and accountability. To Diamond a democracy not only requires elections, but also a) the absence of reserved domains of power for the military or other actors not accountable to the electorate; b) horizontal accountability of office holders constraining the executive power to protect constitutionalism, legality, and the deliberative process; c) extensive provisions for political and civic pluralism, for individuals and group freedoms, so that "contending interests and values may be expressed and compete through ongoing processes of articulation and representation, beyond periodic elections"; and d) the existence of the rule of law in which "all citizens have political and legal equality, and the state and its agents are themselves subject to the law" (Diamond 1999, 11).

This book adopts Diamond's second conception of democracy which, in addition to including elections, requires accountable governments, freedoms, and the rule of law. It is important, however, to keep in mind first, that democracy is an ongoing political process and second, Diamond's distinction between electoral and liberal democracy: Most countries undergoing democratization fall between these two types, they exhibit some but not all the characteristics of a liberal democracy and often more than those of an electoral one.

Although democracy has been analyzed as being part of a process of political transition, less is known about the democratization process in the aftermath of a civil war. There is also little knowledge about the rationales and effect of international actors on democratization processes in post-conflict countries. To explore these questions, this book uses Nicaragua as a case study in which its democratic transition is explored within the contexts of the legacy of war and of international support for democracy. These arguments will develop in relation to already existing studies that provide important but limited accounts of these issues. The study will provide a foundation to advance theoretical considerations about democratization under conditions of a transition from civil war and as an evolving process in which international norms have been advanced to protect and foster democracy.

Chapter 2

International Dimension of Democracy: Trends and Dynamics

International Support for Democracy

The process of democratization around the world starting in the seventies, represents one key political transformation in contemporary history. Since 1974 the number of democracies in the world dramatically increased, constituting what Huntington (1991) called a third wave of democracy. According to Karatnycky (1998, 5), at the beginning of 1998 there were 117 formally established democracies, regimes with multiparty, competitive elections and constitutionally established governments. This number was almost double that of 1988 and a substantial increase from 1993. The spread of democracy is also observed in the political freedoms and civil liberties of countries. Freedom House counted 81 countries as free at the beginning of 1998, a substantial increase from 76 countries in 1994, 53 in 1985, and 42 in 1972. Figure 2.1 shows this trend over time as documented by the PolityIV data (Marshall and Jaggers, 2002).

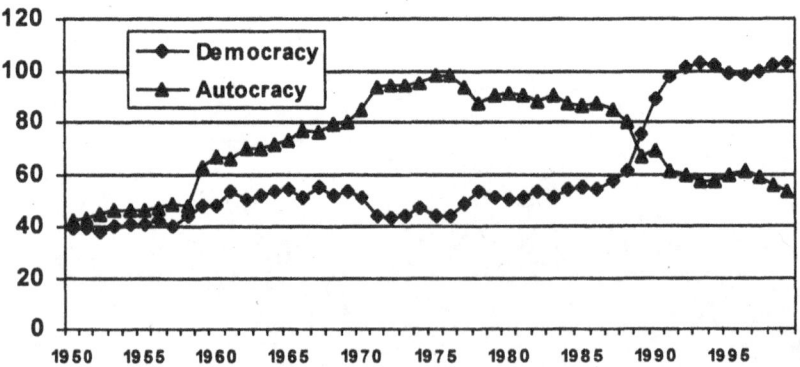

Figure 2.1 Democratization since 1950

The expansion and development of democratization is, in significant part, indicative of a global concern for freer societies (Gruegel 1999, 19). A critical feature observed in the 'global spread of democracy' is the increasing involvement of international actors, who have encouraged democratization at various levels of civil and political society. For this reason, Whitehead (1996, 3) has argued, "we must not overlook the distinctly restrictive international contexts under which the great majority of really existing democracies ('polyarchies') became established, or were re-established." Huntington's *The Third Wave* (1991) explains that external involvement was a critical variable in the third wave of democratization that started in the seventies. In Huntington's (1991, 86-87) opinion,

> by the late 1980s the major sources of power and influence in the world--the Vatican, the European Community, the United States, and the Soviet Union-- were actively promoting liberalization and democratization. Rome delegitimized authoritarian regimes in Catholic countries, Brussels provided incentives for democratization in Southern and eastern Europe; Washington pushed democratization in Latin America; Moscow removed the principal obstacle to democratization in Eastern Europe.

This recent process of democratization dating since the mid-seventies reflects an international dimension, which has taken up greater roles in influencing domestic politics. The international dimension of democracy is the effort of international actors seeking to change or adapt political practices, institutions, laws, and policies in conformity to a model of democracy (Orozco 1995). This influence has occurred in relation to the goals (objectives) and means (mechanisms) employed. In the first case, influence can be exerted to achieve one of two objectives: a) to ensure the success of a particular ongoing issue, or b) to shape the nature and/or outcome of an event. In the second case, the ways or means by which influence is exerted relates to the objectives and the type of international actor. These mechanisms of influence vary in relation to the extent of influence sought, from complete control of a given scenario to the formation of consent.

Specifically, the relationship between the goals and means of international influence is reflected from the interaction of three dynamics. First, in the multiplicity of international actors involved in domestic political processes. Second, in the conditions under which actor involvement with democracy-building activities occurs. Third, in the use of varying forms of international influence.

This international dimension thus means that, although the establishment and consolidation of a democratic regime requires, first and foremost, the participation of internal actors, the commitment of external forces to support and invest resources in democracy, to exert pressures on anti-democratic regimes and to assist newly established democracies has become a key practice and policy in international relations. Moreover, internal actors, whether these are pro- or anti-democracy, can no longer neglect the influence of external agents over democratic issues.

Dynamics of the International Dimension of Democratization

International mobilization to promote democracy has various dynamics. First, states are no longer the only promoters of democracy. A growing number of international civil society organizations actively promote democracy, often as their raison d'etre. Second, the conditions in which this occurs are varied. Third, there is no one single way of encouraging democracy, and these diverse methods are not mutually exclusive. Fourth, the varied areas in which actors invest resources to promote democracy suggest that notions of democracy are complex and not limited to elections.

The international promotion of democracy has become a widespread practice in both scope and intensity in terms of the variety of actors involved, as well as their methods. This point can be demonstrated through an examination of the actors engaged in international democracy promotion and the methods and instruments they employ.

Actors

For many years governments remained the most active promoters of democracy outside their national boundaries. However, as Diamond (1997, 312) argues, states "increasingly share the arena with a wide variety of non-governmental organizations (NGOs)." The post-Cold War period has shown a clearer picture of the array of international actors and of those involved in democracy promotion. Three primary sets of actors actively promote democracy abroad: states, international civil society movements, and international organizations.

States Long-established democracies have been the primary state actors promoting democracy abroad. This category includes two subsets of actors: first, dominant and intermediate powers, that is democratic states which by virtue of their political, economic and military strength have affected the domestic politics of other states which fall within their sphere of influence. Examples of these are France, the United States, Germany, Japan, and Great Britain. Second, less powerful and/or influential democratic states that have made democracy and human rights a major foreign policy issue. These are democracies whose power position is weaker and use diplomacy and reputation among their main policy tools to influence other countries. This latter group includes countries like Canada, Sweden, Norway, Denmark, the Netherlands, and Costa Rica. Most established democracies in the industrialized world have democracy promotion programs in their foreign policy agendas. These programs, as will be observed later, focus on a variety of issues.

In general, it is important to recognize that democratization issues are strongly and primarily influenced by dominant powers, they manipulate the development or course of democracy in a manner that reflects their interests and identities. Countries will implement democratization policies that are consistent with the ethos of their polity. Thus, U.S. foreign policy towards democracy will follow a liberal pattern oriented towards its relationship with individual rights and a market economy and will make use of its strength to prevail in its position. However, this fact does not preclude or guarantee the success of dominant powers. Because of the emerging preeminence and influence non-state groups, international organizations, or lesser dominant states, these often are able to advance alternative strategies to foster democracy.

International civil society movements Scott Turner (1998, 25) argues that two contemporary developments "call into question the traditional conception of governance associated with state sovereignty." The first is the growing strength and power of transnational corporations. The second is the proliferation of national and international non-governmental organizations and social movements, or "global society", which Turner notes has "extended the range of citizen action beyond the institutional parameters of the sovereign state."

Support, or the absence of it, for democratization abroad is not purely the outcome of government decisions; citizens' groups also engage in efforts to support a universal claim for democracy. Citizens increasingly recognize that anything that happens inside or outside their borders may, or will, affect their lives, thus heightening an awareness of living in an interdependent world. Appreciation of the global has raised 'cosmopolitan' sensitivities among people to the point that, either as public opinion or organized constituencies, citizens have prompted democratic change around the world. As Parry (1992, 148) argues, these acts are "evidence of an incipient cosmopolitan citizenship." This sensitivity towards the rest of the world has been fundamentally influenced by the development of communication and information technology, which connects people with any part of the world in a matter of seconds, minutes, or hours, depending on the degree of material connection desired (Gamble 1993, 323).

Moreover, an increased number of civil society groups have effectively organized into foreign affairs advocacy organizations designed to promote democracy, human rights, development, environmental protection, and other sets of issues aimed at attaining the welfare of the rest of the world. The involvement of international non-governmental organizations is relatively recent and has coincided with the process of democratization and concern with the fate of developing countries. These organizations mobilize their forces to demand participation in world affairs, either through their own achieved and coordinated organized involvement or through their national governments. Figure 2.2 shows the significant increase in the number of international NGOs working in the past twenty years.

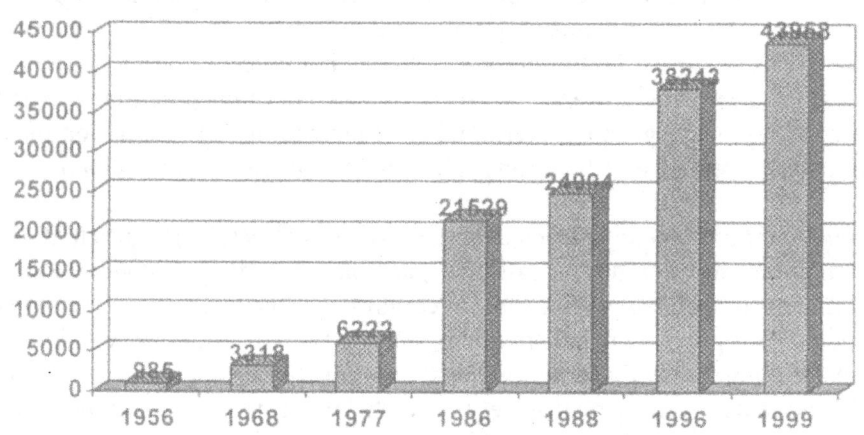

Figure 2.2 Rise of International NGOs, 1956-1999

The involvement of civil society organizations in international affairs has led to increased democratization in the making of foreign policy as new constituencies mobilize their interests. As Moreno (1990, 14) comments in the United States the case of "an 'alternative foreign policy establishment' has been formed that includes churches and human rights groups, business associations, single-issue solidarity groups, and at times, the media. These organizations have focused their efforts on both public and private diplomacy." Thus, many organizations and individuals have also assumed transnational roles. This process of transnationalization of activities develop not only out of the awareness of interdependence, that what happens *here* has repercussions *there,* but also from the realization that the experiences suffered *here* are very similar to the experiences suffered *there.* Both NGOs and advocacy movements have engaged in developing strategies across borders in different issues.

These organizations have facilitated democracy and conflict resolution in many places, even in cases in which states were unable to do so. In fact, as Mawlawi (1992, 392) notes, despite the fact that these organizations lack the leverage of states, "they do possess certain enabling characteristics, particular to their non-governmental nature, that enhance their ability to contribute to a more enduring peace." For example, human rights organizations like Amnesty International and Human Rights Watch and environmental movements such as Greenpeace have been successful in promoting social change or stopping violence. These actors mainly work across national boundaries; their advocacy of social change and the attention they bring to issues or problems not often addressed by official policy makers gives primary salience to democracy.

Another important sector of international civil society is diasporic or exile movements. As Yossi Shain (1995, 812) contends, "the third wave of democratic transitions have awakened older diasporas in the United States and energized the more recently organized ethnic groups. Both of these groups now play an increasingly important role in providing support for democratization and self-determination abroad." Such groups have become more influential in international affairs. Shain goes on to claim that diasporic communities have contributed significantly to democratic change in their homelands.

> They do so by challenging the home regime's international legitimacy, exposing human rights violations, combating the home regime's foreign propaganda, obstructing friendly relations with the United States through effective lobbies, and finally assisting and actively participating in the struggle of the domestic opposition. In many instances political exiles and other diaspora members have returned home in the aftermath of regime transition to occupy top private and public posts. (Shain 1995, 830)

It is important to stress that any of these external forces (international NGOs, states, diasporas) act in close connection with local opposition forces in the non-democratic regime. The greater the international connection of local opposition forces, the greater the international support for democratization. In this case, democracy, human rights groups, and diasporas have played a major role in transmitting information about current conditions in a non-democracy (Sikkink 1996).

International Organizations International organizations (IOs) such as the United Nations or the Organization of American States are institutions created predominantly by states to carry out a mandate. As institutions they prescribe behavior, constrain activity, and shape expectation through the use of rules (Ruggie 1988). Although they follow a mandate, they may also become autonomous agents of international action. This independence is observed in their capacity to apply meaning to their actions through new rules and also to monitor and exert pressure on their members.

IOs have grown in number since World War II and have come to be an embodiment of international regimes; that is, they have evolved into "institutions with explicit rules, agreed upon by governments, that pertain to particular sets of issues in international relations" (Keohane 1989, 4). Rosenau (1997, 387) asserts "international organizations (IOs), and especially the United Nations, serve as bridges across the frontier that separates states in the state-centric world and NGOs and other actors in the multi-centric world."

The role of international organizations in democratization is an important development of the post-Cold War period. These institutions are increasingly involved in issues that respond to human rights violations and warfare. Because of their increased participation and expanded decision-making roles in these kinds of activities, their influence has increased tremendously. Since the end of the Cold War, IOs have monitored elections around the world and facilitated and followed the political democratization process, as well as provided training and assistance. Moreover, international organizations have coordinated efforts to establish normative practices about human rights, democratization, and conflict resolution.

Conditions in which Democracy Promotion Occurs

International involvement in democratization takes place in at least four kinds of instances. Whitehead (1987) identifies three of these contexts or international dimensions for the promotion of democracy. One occurs when pressures on undemocratic governments to democratize is applied by international actors. Examples of this condition or context are Nicaragua under Somoza and after 1987, Haiti after the overthrow of Aristide, Chile under Pinochet, Argentina under the military junta before 1982, South Africa during the Apartheid system, and Panama under Noriega. A second category involves international support for fledgling democracies attempting to consolidate. Relevant cases here include Nicaragua after the 1990 elections,

El Salvador after the 1991 peace negotiations, and South Africa after the end of apartheid. A third situation occurs when global pressure is maintained against anti-democratic forces. This last case occurs more often than the previous two and operates in rhetorical forms as well as through specific policies. These stances against recalcitrant forces are observed, for example, in the cases of Haiti, the death squads in Guatemala and El Salvador, right-wing terrorist attacks in South Africa, the killing of students in China during the 1989 democracy movement, and in African countries' demands for the extension of civil rights and equality to black Americans in the United States in the 1950s and 1960s. These three international initiatives in support of democracy often interact with each other to demand either political opening (liberalization) or enhance (consolidate) democracy.

There is, however, a fourth case in which international actors become involved in democratization issues. In this case, international actors seek to promote democratic change by means other than the narrowly political. Examples of facilitating democracy in this sense include promoting economic development, humanitarian assistance, and environmental support. These forms of democratic promotion are especially tangible and proactive. Many international actors recognize that addressing social and economic issues is fundamental to achieving democracy, and that freedom and the rule of law need to be accompanied by advances in social justice. Thus, United Nations development programs as well as some official development assistance provided by bilateral donors have been used as mechanisms to strengthen democracy. Relief efforts to help rebuild countries affected by internal disasters have often been linked to a stage in which the fragility of the democratic system may collapse.

Pressures on undemocratic governments In the seventies, international actors mobilized to pressure countries to democratize and so to join the "community" of democratic nations. The number of undemocratic countries in the world in the 1960s was high; most of Latin America, Asia, and Africa suffered the violation of at least one, and usually a number, of the criteria used to define a procedural minimum of democracy. Political power was particularly monopolized by the military.

In this context, Sikkink (1993, 415) argues that international pressure to improve human rights improvements were met with a continuum of responses, from the delinquent country's denial and refusal to cooperate with demands for human rights protection, to formal but not substantive acceptance of the legitimacy of international human rights practices, i.e., from paying lip service to cooperating with regime changes. In some cases the demands stopped at one point of the continuum, and in other cases this continuum was interrupted by the use of force, as in the case of the U.S. invasion of Panama.

A case in point is that of Nicaragua during the Somoza dictatorship and pressures from the Inter-American community. In 1978 the Inter-American Commission for Human Rights urged the international community to stop the genocide committed by Anastasio Somoza in its repression against Nicaraguans. As a result, the OAS voted in favor of a resolution in which it called for "the immediate replacement of the Somoza regime, installation of a democratic government, guarantee and respect for human rights and the holding of free elections." The OAS statement was praised by the Inter-American Commission on Human Rights saying that "for the first time in the history of the OAS, and perhaps in the history of any international organization, the resolution deprived an incumbent government of a member State of the Organization to legitimacy, based on the human rights violations committed by that government against its own population." This decision by the OAS decision not only paved the way to overthrow the Somoza dictatorship, but also displayed earlier signs and indication for a future decisive commitment to promote democracy among its member States.

International calls for democracy follow a similar trend to that for human rights, with the international community exerting pressure in order to achieve political change in a non-democracy. International pressures often occur in situations in which external actors perceive the severity of the political crisis as intolerable, or when domestic forces appeal for international support to bring about democratic change. In many instances international pressures concentrate in achieving political opening, or liberalization, prior to having an authoritarian government hold elections. This action is perceived as a key strategy to gradually move a regime into a democratization path. Dalpino (2000, 4) stresses along these lines that "the gradual nature and incremental pace of liberalization offers the possibility of combining some degree of stability with political change." The following are examples of the use of international pressure.

Under the Franco dictatorship, Spain received international pressure from European countries, especially members of the European Economic Community (EEC), to become democratic. Although these external pressures were not the main cause of democracy in Spain, two important international factors helped to accelerate the process of democratic transition. First, support for Spain's internal opposition from communist and social democratic parties and other advocacy movements proved to be important in strengthening "intermestic" ties against Franco. These pressures consisted of statements by external political parties rating the state of human rights, and mobilization of forces to pressure countries (Germany and France, in particular) to demand democratization in Spain. Such actions moved the Franco dictatorship from denying the need for democratic change to conceding some political changes. Second, EEC member countries pressured Spain through a process of political conditionality, by making Spain's democratization a condition of its membership in the EEC. Spaniards wished to assert their European identity, an identity perceived moreover as modern and democratic. Although in the 1970s Spain's economy was still behind the rest of Europe, there was a pragmatic assumption that a Spain linked to Europe would develop faster. These issues played a fundamental role in the process of transition to democracy in Spain.

In contrast to Spain, most of the post-World War II Latin American governments could be regarded as semi-democracies (Diamond 1996) or delegative democracies (O'Donnell 1990, 56). These systems exhibit some democratic elements but might be missing others such as full protection of rights and freedoms, abuses, fraud, or undue military influence in the government. Despite being regarded as democratic and politically stable, Panama's political system, for example, was characterized as having a fragile party system, pacted elections, "caudillo" politics, and military presence in key political decisions. In the mid-eighties, Panama's semi-democracy suffered a series of crises including the sudden death of General Omar Torrijos, political realignment within the Army, the emergence of General Manuel A. Noriega in charge of the Army, and economic crisis. The end result was that the Army gained direct control of the country, which in turn led to the manipulation of both elections and civilian power. The involvement of the head of the Army with drug trafficking and human rights violations, and the use of security forces to intimidate opposition leaders, increased tension within and outside the country. Gradually, Panama started to lose international legitimacy and credibility. Further, it directly alienated the United States, its most important ally and the strongest power in the hemisphere. During the 1989 electoral campaign, the countries belonging to the Inter-American system pressured the Panamanian government, with General Noriega as the de facto president, to offer opposition parties guarantees of a fair election as well as to protect the civil and political rights of all citizens. The government, however, annulled the elections, and thus increased international tension still further (Smith 1992, 229). The OAS' inability to bring democracy back to Panama plus American pressures on Noriega led to the invasion of Panama by United States forces. The U.S. justified the attack as aiming to restore democracy and to try Noriega on drug trafficking charges. Restoration of civilian rule opened the opportunity for democratization in the country. The use of external military force did not, however, eliminate corruption. Nevertheless, in the subsequent five years the country slowly entered a phase of democratization strengthened by the 1994 elections.

One case in which international demands for democratization were successful in stopping human rights abuses was Argentina. After the 1976 military coup, the Army resorted to the practice of "disappearances" as a way to deny the existence of political prisoners or repression. In response, an international network of human rights organizations such as Amnesty International, countries like the United States and some European nations, IOs such as the Organization of American States pressured the government to stop disappearances.

An initial strategy used by some opponents of the Argentine junta like the Mothers of Plaza de Mayo consisted of documenting abuses and making them public around the world (Schirmer 1993, 32). The objective consisted of drawing collective support to force the government to stop the killing, a common position accepted by most international actors. For example, in 1977 the United States began to link the resumption of foreign economic and military aid to human rights improvement. In this context, the Inter-American commission for Human Rights visited the country, reported on the conditions, and called for changes in the regime. Growing pressure from the "international variable", the term the military used, was affecting the government and increased the costs of continued violations. Although the transition to democracy did not start until 1983, most abuses had declined by1980 (Sikkink 1993).

South Africa is a case study in international mobilization that pressured the Pretoria regime to change its racially based system. Prior to 1990, South Africa caused international political debate over the ways to condemn and end its practice of Apartheid. From the time the Nationalist Party assumed power in 1948 and began the institutionalization of Apartheid, the United Nations condemned the regime's racial system and its associated discrimination. South Africa was isolated and confronted by many international actors with different stakes in the country and its democratization. For over forty years, pressures on South Africa's regime were implemented in different ways. Despite such pressures, the concerted effort to make South Africa change lasted for a very long time. Four issues around which international actors mobilized in light of their varied interests characterized the process of putting pressure on the government to end Apartheid.

First, despite the fact that there was an international uproar against the Apartheid regime, Cold War issues proved to have greater international salience than racism. The Pretoria regime was able to capitalize on the Cold War issue by ostensibly transforming its Apartheid ideology into an anti-communist foreign policy. Thus, the regime was able to neutralize some countries and gain some diplomatic support, including from the United States under Reagan, by invoking anti-communist stances. However, as the Cold War faded and political resistance against racism and repression grew and became clearer to all international actors and their respective internal constituencies, the relative and conditional support changed in favor of ending Apartheid (Baker 1989).

Second, despite the denial of civil and political rights to non-white South Africans and gross human rights abuses primarily against the black population, there were mixed and confusing signals about how to challenge South Africa. Support for sanctions against South Africa by many Western countries, the most effective group in promoting an end to Apartheid, was constrained by a belief that economic development on its own would gradually erode Apartheid. (Not to mention that economic sanctions would negatively affect employment in the sanctioning countries.) Although in one way or another most countries criticized South Africa, a consensus on the desirability of sanctions, which was led by the Nordic countries, the American black caucus and other international organizations, took a concerted collective effort (Klotz 1994).

Third, the geographic location of South Africa and its isolation from the direct sphere of influence of major powers contributed to prolonging the struggle against Apartheid. As Vale (1991, 63) argues, "the sheer ability of the minority to sustain its position for a long period of time was directly proportional to South Africa's distance from an alternative political message." Once a "multinational" effort was consolidated against South Africa, world hegemony was substituted for the lack of a powerful regional pressure.

Finally, it took a combination of means and multi-pronged strategies and the aid of many actors to increase the costs to Pretoria of maintaining its regime. By the mid-eighties, South Africa was practically isolated in almost all aspects of international life. Diplomatically, the country had very little representation: it was banned from participating in many cultural activities, militarily, South Africa lacked allies, and trade sanctions were affecting the economy, (Vale, 1991). While the international community isolated South Africa diplomatically, progressive donor countries identified and aided both political society and civil society groups in an effort to maintain internal anti-apartheid pressure (Landsberg, 2000, p.107). After many years of international pressure and foreign support for internal activist movements, the Pretoria regime engaged in a transition process that started to give hope to the country and international recognition to the reformation leaders. In fact, as Ottoway (1993, 210) notes, "by the government's own admission, sanctions did contribute to change."

Mexico provides a case study of pro-democracy actors seeking out international support for their efforts. After the 1988 elections and protests against electoral fraud, actors mobilized to demand political change and greater democracy in Mexico. Keck and Sikkink (1998) say that during this period "human rights consciousness began to penetrate civil society. In 1984 only four human rights NGOs existed in Mexico; seven years later there were thirty, and by 1993 there were more than two hundred. International attention helped create the political space within which this growth was possible." These organizations established networks with organizations outside Mexico in order to bring international attention, especially from the United States, to their cause. As a result, two major international actions regarding Mexico occurred in the 1990s. First, human rights organizations, labor movements, environmental organizations, and political leaders in the United States demanded that the Mexican government defend workers' rights and improve labor conditions. For example, an organization monitoring human rights in Mexico, the Minnesota Advocates for Human Rights, worked closely with local groups, but also engaged in documenting and publicizing rights violations in the early nineties. This organization had not only made people outside Mexico aware of delicate rights conditions in the country but had warned of the possibility of the Chiapas indigenous uprising in January 1994 (Scott 1993, 6; Illif 1993, 34A). Second, Mexico faced growing pressure to comply with election results and to restrain from practicing electoral fraud. As a result the government relaxed its electoral laws, opened up investigations into human rights abuses, recognized the need to improve social conditions for minorities and allowed international observer missions to the country. As is true in most cases, the process of change has primarily been an internal one. Nevertheless, international influence has become an important element enabling democratization in Mexico.

International support for fledging democracies In addition to applying pressure to democratize, international actors have also helped to create and consolidate new democracies. This practical assistance often involves the direct participation of international actors. Whereas democracy may be urged in a push for fair elections or protection of human rights, international actors who provide policy advice, train officials to organize elections, monitor elections, fund civil society organizations and improve the justice system may actually facilitate it (Carothers 1999). Support to help consolidate democratic transitions often occurs when international actors have established a commitment to continue their involvement in democratizing a country or when they perceive an opportunity to offer assistance that will be more effective than in situations of crisis.

Moving beyond mere pressure to directly enabling democracies explains why the international community continued its involvement in South

Africa after Pretoria lifted its ban on the ANC, freed Nelson Mandela, and began to end Apartheid. The relationship between the U.S. and South Africa as well as South Africa's links with other countries and organizations were transformed from confrontation and isolation to international cooperation. The participation of the international community after Mandela's release took place within the context of the negotiations towards a transition to a non-racial democracy. United Nations participation in the national peace agreements facilitated agreement among opposing parties and helped to reduce conflict and violence. The UN sent monitors to South Africa to observe the negotiations, prevent conflict, and strengthen the agreements (Gastrow 1995, 72-73). These actions were accompanied by the mobilization of other actors, such as the Organization of African Unity and the European Community. However, as Landsberg (1994b, 9) argues about negotiations in South Africa, "attempts to shape the nature of the settlement were also evident." The Clinton administration tried to influence the debate on South Africa's future political system, by pointing to problems in establishing a federal system for the country and conditioning aid packages to agreements on an election date. Election missions by international observers also had an important impact on the transition process by offering guarantees to the population and bringing legitimacy to the process. In general, not only did the international community seek to consolidate the transition through procedural observation (monitoring elections), negotiating peace agreements, and political dialogue, but international donors also prioritized "working with the government and civil society to make the new democratic institutions viable and secure, and ensuring the success of the transition to full majority full in the 1999 elections" (Landsberg, 119-120).

After peace negotiations in El Salvador in 1991, the transition to democracy included reforming the justice system and the Army, investigating past human rights abuses, establishing a national forum on the economy, and organizing national elections. Two major international actors, the United States and UN, played a fundamental role in helping to implement these goals. The United States, as a regional power that had influenced the fate of the country during the civil war, helped to neutralize the Army when it tried to end compliance with the agreements. During the peace negotiations, the United States conditioned the release of military and economic aid to improvements in human rights and argued that if impunity over violations persisted, it would withdraw its assistance. This act led military chiefs to comply with the agreement, which devalued the retirement of military officers implicated in human rights abuses (Montgomery 1995, 221-222). The U.S. position also warned the government to be more serious about the new political process. The United Nations, an actor mandated to facilitate the negotiations, participated in the peace process by mediating, monitoring human rights and disarmament, and helping to design a development agenda for the post-civil war period (Wilkins 1997). Its support for democratic transition was amplified by development assistance policies and by the UN's status as an international voice respected by the government. More important the UN's institutional presence in El Salvador gave great credibility to the political process (Johnstone 1995).

Both the United States and United Nations contributed to the March 1994 elections, not only through monitoring and training, but also as external forces guaranteeing the safety of opposition parties from death squads. El Salvador's progress towards democratization as influenced by international actors constitutes one of the most important success stories in contemporary international relations. In fact, the international dimension of democracy expressed in the mobilization of many international actors, mostly led by the UN and United States, and the articulation of different policy strategies of democratization was successful in slowly bringing normalcy and democracy to the country.

Stands against anti-democratic forces Standing up against anti-democratic forces is a common practice of governments and other international actors and is a key dimension of the international campaign for democracy. These stands usually occur in the context of criticizing a regime. Reports of undemocratic practices of particular forces, or poor ratings of the degree of democraticity of a country may, for example, lead to international actors sending investigative missions. This dimension highlights contrasting views among international actors about the perceptions of anti-democratic forces. For example, during the democratic transitions European countries were more critical of the undemocratic actions of Latin American regimes, than was the United States, which perceived communism, not repression, as the real threat to democracy.

Stands against anti-democratic forces may involve lesser or greater international commitment than do the other two dimensions of promoting democracy, pressure and support. When the democracy movement emerged in China in the late eighties and the government responded with what could be called an asymmetrical display of force, the international community protested against such repression. However, China resisted international protests. A more successful example was the international stand for civil liberties for minorities in the former Soviet Union. Under sustained international pressure, the USSR gave Jews the right to practice their religion and to enjoy the rights of emigration. The USSR was not the only superpower to be challenged in this fashion. Another interesting case is the stance taken in African countries and elsewhere against racial discrimination in the United States in the sixties. After World War II, the United States came under sustained international focus and pressure to extend democracy to black Americans, especially those in the southern states. In the critical ***Brown v. Board of Education*** Supreme Court case that found school segregation unconstitutional, the Court was specifically motivated by international opinion against segregation. Pressure against racism in the 1950s and 1960s, especially from the newly independent African countries, challenged the United States to end a double standard by which it pursued diplomatic relations with non-white nations but segregated African-Americans at home (Layton 1999).

Countries that undermine democracy and human rights threaten those who attempt to take a stand against them. A case in point was the international human rights movement's efforts to promote change and protect the human rights of the people of East Timor. Indonesia's forced annexation of East Timor in 1976 was followed by systematic repression and ethnocide of the population. In June 1994, an Asia-Pacific Conference on East Timor was organized in Manila to study ways to protect the rights of the East Timor population and bring international attention to the island and to Indonesia's abuses. Despite Indonesia's forcible attempts to undermine/prevent the conference by threatening the Philippine government, the human rights community responded with condemnation and protest. The conference not only went ahead, but focused international attention on Indonesia's illegal practices (Time 1994, 41).

Democracy by other means International mobilization for democracy occurs not only when political issues are at stake. Severe refugee crises, economic turmoil or environmental disasters also mobilize international actors to help protect democracy. Official development assistance provided by international aid agencies is a key tool for democratization. Donor countries stress the strong relationship between democracy and aid under different conditions. One example of democratization by other means has been the support for economic reconstruction after the natural disaster caused in 1998 by Hurricane Mitch in Central America, Honduras and Nicaragua in particular. In responding to the emergency caused by the hurricane, donor countries and organizations formed a Consultative Group, which prepared a long-term reconstruction plan as a strategy to support the economic and political changes happening in the region. The consultative group not only presented Central America with a reconstruction package, but it required governments to consult with civil society about reconstruction strategies. The group also advanced ideas and policies about transparency and good governance in the administration of funds.

Moreover, support for community action groups, media, educational organizations, is a means by which the international community can attempt to fortify those actors within a particular state who seek to safeguard political stability—by acting within the rule of law--while simultaneously advocating and representing the needs of various populations within a state. For example, international actors, such as the Ford Foundation and the Asia Foundation, fund the Philippine Center for Investigative Journalism, an organization which has been instrumental in promoting gender legislation, protecting and strengthening environmental legislation, and blocking corrupt appointments to government positions (Golub 2000, 138). Civil society groups has enabled citizens to influence change at the national level, and funding for civil society groups is a poignant means for the international community to influence democratization.

Mechanisms

The international support for democracy is through the use of certain mechanisms or strategies designed to provoke change in a country. These mechanisms are employed with the objective of ensuring policy success or shaping the nature and outcome of issues. Actors options may range between support in creating a democratic consensus within a country, to condition any form of cooperation or democratization, to challenge a country's policies in an adversarial manner, or to exercise control over that country by force According to Whitehead (1996) there are three mechanisms that explain the international dimension of democracy. These are contagion, control, and consent. Contagion refers to the ways in which geographic proximity affects democratization. Control refers to exporting democracy by means of some form of force (violence, threat of violence, extreme diplomatic pressure) by some dominant actor. Consent refers to the promotion of democracy by agreement and means other than force. Although these three methods are not mutually exclusive and sometimes can overlap, the recent wave of democracy, in Whitehead's opinion, falls primarily into this latter category. To these categories, Schmitter (1996) adds a fourth, conditionality. Conditonality refers to the ability of international organizations or donor countries to condition their support (financial, political, or diplomatic) on democratic governance. I add a fifth category to Whitehead and Schimitter's classification, namely that of open challenge to a regime. This category particularly applies to diasporic movements and other militant organizations that, once in exile, actively attempt to influence the political processes in their homelands in open defiance of the ruling regimes.

Contagion, control, consent, conditionality, and challenge are five mechanisms actors resort to in order to influence political outcomes in another country. Of these five, four have been associated with (but not limited to) specific actors: a) regional powers influence democratic processes by control, b) bilateral and multilateral 'democratic conditionality' policies act as mechanisms of compliance, c) non-state actors intervene as agents of consent and as contributors to help create and/or protect domestic democratic forces, and d) exile diasporas defy the established order.

Control by regional powers In international relations, the act of exerting direct influence on the internal affairs of another country is identified as one of control and is generally linked to geopolitical constraints. Geopolitics refers to the relations of power among international actors as they try to influence their interests and identity. Indeed, this desire to affect others lies at the heart of politics, which is at the heart of disputes "over claims to the authority to describe, interpret, explain, or prescribe some aspect of the nature of reality" (Edwards 1992, 8). Because democracy is largely a political construct, competing claims over the meaning of democracy are regular occurrence in international relations. Thus, international actors, regional powers in particular, seek to legitimate their claims by exercising power, through discourse and/or force and wish to make certain that their claims to authority over an aspect of reality (or the whole of reality) become the norm. In this context, geopolitics played a major role in defining a model of democracy for Nicaragua, characterized by the United States control of its sphere of influence. Compliance with the dominant actor's claims was achieved by coercion or because the norms that underscore or justify that compliance have been internalized or recognized as legitimate by the country that is the object of control and international community.

Geopolitical control plays an important role in the process of promoting democracy. The dominant external country strongly and primarily influences reconciliation between a particular perspective on democracy and a universal one. Whitehead (1987, 39) argues that "it is the regionally dominant countries that have the most scope to set the terms of the debate [on democracy], and to define which forces are worthy of support and which deserve exclusion." Although scope does not always mean exclusive or decisive influence, dominant powers give specific support to democracy. In fact, despite European and Latin American involvement/encouragement, it was mainly the United States that set the tone for urging elections in Nicaragua in 1990.

This point is fundamental insofar as dominant powers manipulate the development or course of democracy. It is important to bear in mind the historical component of power relations and its relationship to democracy. Most industrialized Western countries had established patterns of colonial relations in developing countries. After the independence movements in former colonies, first world countries maintained their dominance through cultural, economic, and political influence. They created spheres of influence in the areas that had previously been under their colonial control and expected these domains to be respected by other regional or international powers. American control resided mainly in the Western Hemisphere, whereas Europe's domain was Asia and Africa. As the United States grew in power after World War II, its influence as a major world power increased, and American control of, or at least pervasive influence in, the life of Third World countries was unavoidable.

Influence and control of regional powers does not always encourage the use of force. Economic pressures and diplomatic efforts may suffice for a country to obtain compliance. However, the likelihood of using force grows when there is a high level of tension between the two countries or when the regional power finds force preferable to non-coercive means.

Promoting consent A main role for international actors is to contribute to (or impede) the consensus upon which new democracies must be based. A "democratic regime", notes Whitehead (1996,15), "requires the positive support and involvement of a wide range of social and political groupings, support that must be sustained over a considerable period and in the face of diverse uncertainties. Such support must be more or less freely given for the term 'democracy' to apply." Whitehead's study represents the most comprehensive analysis of the role of the international contest in promoting democracy. At the very least, this study highlights the external actors as agents creating incentives for consent, as well as helping to create or form opposition forces.[2] Whitehead points to four aspects of international processes that contribute (or impede) the generation of consent in new democracies:

> (1) the territorial limits to successive democratizations and their consequences for established alliance systems; (2) the main international structures tending to generate consent for such regime changes; (3) the ways in which authentic national democratic actors may be constituted from

---

[2] Whitehead's study represents the most comprehensive analysis of the role of the international context in promoting democracy. The study highlights the actors as agents creating incentives for consent, as well as helping to create or assist democratic forces.

relatively diffuse transnational groupings; (4) the role of
international demonstration effects (1996, 16).

Referring to the international structures that tend to generate consent, Whitehead argues that national opposition forces are likely to have external origins as exile clusters (as in the Chilean case) or social opposition movements that enjoy some degree of international protection through religious groups, human rights organizations, or political parties. He further adds that a sign of autonomy of opposition forces in the political process occurs when democratic movements no longer receive close support from abroad. To Whitehead this new independence is a central part of democratization and concerns the "interactive process by which the external supporters of the various contending political factions step (or are driven) back, relinquishing leverage over their proteges, and lifting vetoes against their competitors."

Philippe Schmitter agrees with Whitehead that a process of diffusion, or in Whitehead's term, contagion, produces waves of democratization. Schmitter adds that as diffusion further increases with each instance of democratization, another momentum emerges that is influenced by consent. This momentum contributes to develop non-governmental organizations and informal networks devoting their activities to promote human rights, protect minorities, monitor elections, "all intended to further democratization"(Schmitter 1996, 38). In consequence, a variety of foreign non-state actors 'intervene' to promote or protect democracy. Thus, Schmitter adds,

> the international context surrounding democratization has shifted from a primary reliance on public, inter-governmental channels of influence towards an increased involvement of private, non-governmental organizations—and it is the concrete activity of these agents of consent, rather than the abstract process of contagion, that accounts for the global reach of regime change (1996, 39).

Conditionality and international organizations The articulation of international interests in democratization often operates in the context of issue linkages by which an international actor's policy requires a particular policy change in the undemocratic country. Linkage diplomacy is a strategy that makes one actor's policy contingent on the behavior of another state's policy. Such influence projects a kind of power that intends to produce a set of outcomes favorable to the actors demanding them (Li 1993, 350). More recently such a strategy has been labeled as conditionality, or democratic conditionality.

"Democratic conditionality" is a common strategy of international pressure. It is a key thesis of Whitehead and Schmitter, as well as of Linz and Stepan (1996) who identify it as diffusion. As democracy and the market system spread throughout the world, non-democracies are left more vulnerable to external pressures. International actors (states and international institutions) condition the terms of their relationships (belonging to an organization, recognition and legitimacy, and financial or technical assistance) with non-democracies on compliance with certain norms or practices: democracy, good governance, and opposing corruption. For example, as mentioned earlier, international financial institutions condition their cooperation to good governance in the recipient country (Manin 1996). Similarly, institutions like the Organization of American States have created institutional mechanisms such as the Unit for the Promotion of Democracy to monitor democratic compliance among the member states. Being a democracy has gradually become a requisite for active membership in the OAS (Acevedo 1996).

Democratic conditionality raises the issue of vulnerability vis-à-vis the international context. With the expanded process of globalization and the spread of democratic views, undemocratic countries have become especially susceptible or vulnerable to external pressures to democratize, particularly when such pressures are conditioned to certain regime needs. Vulnerability refers to the degree of dependence a country has on external actors and its ability (or bargaining power) to manage such dependence. Thus, the success of democratic conditionality policies will be related to the level of external dependence a country has with the world. Richardson (1978, 71-86) describes four kinds of dependence, each associated with a level of vulnerability to external pressure: compliance, decreasing marginal compliance, defiance, and deteriorating compliance. In this context, because of Soviet assistance and diplomatic support in the first half of the eighties, the Sandinistas were less dependent of the U.S.. This situation allowed them to be more defiant of U.S. pressures (Vanderlaan 1986). However, in relation to the rest of the international community, Nicaragua tended to be more compliant due to the fact that the country had increased its dependence on an array of international actors. Democratic conditionality was thus a key pressure on the Sandinistas to hold elections.

Instruments

The four mechanisms employed by international actors to effect change involve various policy instruments, used independently or in tandem with each other.

These instruments are, rhetorical sanction (statements, ratings, and advocacy of democracy), economic pressure (sanctions, suspension of aid, economic blockades, boycotts, or denial of foreign assistance from financial organizations), diplomatic action (actions by diplomats, political and religious leaders or groups, and other advocacy group leaders), material support for democratic forces (electoral training, civic education, human rights monitoring), military action (direct intervention, training, aid, funding of rebel forces), and multilateral diplomacy (UN, OAS, OAU, and the efforts of other organizations). Diamond (1997) groups these instruments into three categories: political assistance, economic assistance, and diplomatic conditionality and sanctions. In either case, although these instruments are contingent on the mechanisms employed, they target specific areas of democracy. These instruments reflect the preferences of international actors and concerns for certain issues such as institution building, civil society, elections, local development or socio-economic development. Choices among the instruments suggest that 'electoralism', or the linkage of democracy to free and fair universal suffrage, is only one aspect of the international dimension of democracy--albeit perhaps the most widely accepted.

Is there a pattern or relationship among the actors, conditions, and mechanisms for international action for democracy? The literature does not suggest the existence of a discernible pattern. One observed tendency relates to the intensity of involvement of regional powers during the early stages of a transition, that is, during the stage in which the conditions for international pressure are met (increased repression, deep economic crisis, or widespread violence). A regional power becomes more involved and compromises its interests more during this stage. However, Schmitter (1996, 49) advances the hypothesis that the "presence of a powerful democratic superpower (or powers) in the regional environment of a given country will have less of an impact upon the consolidation of democracy than the presence of a viable, expanding multilateral international organization." It is important to add to this postulate the presence of various non-state actors who have also exerted substantive influence on the political development of a democracy. In this sense, Schmitter's hypothesis is critical in so far as it appreciates the new roles of regional organizations and raises important questions about the assumptions of regional powers' dominance.

To summarize, the facets of the international dimension of democracy are observed in terms of the variety of actors, conditions, mechanisms, and instruments employed to promote democratic political change in a given country. Although no clear-cut patterns are observed in the literature, these facets are interrelated and both actors and conditions determine the instruments and mechanisms of influence employed in the quest for democratization. There is also a relationship between the degree of democratization and the influence of international actors, that is, as a more stable pattern of democratization ensues, the number of actors increases. Table 2.1 shows an illustration of the relationship among the various factors analyzed here.

Table 2.1 Actors, Mechanisms and Conditions for Mobilization

Condition / Actor	Pressure	Support	Stand	Other
Regional power	Control	Control	Challenge	Consent
Established democracy	Challenge	Consent	Condition	Consent
Neighboring state	Contagion/Challenge.	Contagion	___	Consent
International organization	Condition/Challenge	Consent	Condition	Consent
International civil society (NGOs, diasporas)	Challenge/Consent	Consent	Challenge	Consent

Chapter 3

The Emergence of an International Norm for Democratization

Why do international actors become involved in democratization processes in other countries despite their adherence to the principle of sovereignty in international relations? Democracy promotion (or the lack thereof) nowadays constitutes a mandate among international actors that requires explanation. Little attention has been paid to this question, however, perhaps in part due to the slowness of comparative politics to recognize that the international context influences processes traditionally part of this field. Moreover, until recently, the international relations discipline did not address issues of a traditionally domestic nature (civil conflict, democracy, and the environment, for example) that nevertheless shapes and informs global politics.

This chapter offers an answer to the question raised above and adds to the nascent study of international norms in the international relations discipline. The emergence of an international norm of support for democracy has influenced international actors' decisions to implicate themselves in democratization tasks in countries or regions outside their borders. To support this point, the article first reviews the spread of democracy and the role of international actors. Second, the theory of norms, particularly as it pertains to international relations, is elaborated. The third section identifies the emergence of the norm of democratic entitlement as the key variable explaining international mobilization. Finally, the article explores the limitations of the democratic norm and sovereignty in the global era.

Norms in International Relations

There is at best a small literature explaining the rationale behind international mobilization for democracy. Although comparative political studies paid extensive attention to the conditions under which transitions to democracy occur, their work did not analyze why international actors mobilize to promote democracy. To the credit of this field, however, a few scholars, such as Whitehead (1987; 1996), Lowenthal (1991), Huntington (1991) and Diamond

(1993), recognized international action as a factor explaining democratization, although the rationales for this politics was not addressed. Moreover, studies concerned with democratic theory have traditionally focused on democracy within the boundaries of the state. Political theories have largely neglected the development of a philosophical understanding of democratic impulses across borders (Archibugi and Held 1995, Held 1995).

Realism, traditionally the dominant perspective in international relations, portrayed facts as determined or divided along the lines of a continuum between "material interests and ethical ideals" (Klotz 1995, 13). This dichotomization of social activity has proven inaccurate. Social life is structured instead by a continued (or dialectic) interplay between symbols and matter that constitute social facts. Norms, defined as shared "understandings of standards for behavior" (Klotz 1995, 14), are types of institutionalized facts that result from the interaction among social groups and their intention to conform to some standard of behavior.

Recent approaches concerning norms and ideas in international relations have improved our understandings of international interaction (Kubalkova 1998). They have shown that international norms have consequences and implications for international action. James Rosenau (1997, 180) argues, for example, that the foreign-domestic frontier (that space shared by both domestic and international issues) is a place in which norms continuously operate. He points out that "the most conspicuous indicator of norms shared along the Frontier is the large degree to which it has become commonplace to refer to the concerns and interests of an entity called 'the international community.'" Reference to this community "gives voice to the collective nature of shared challenges." Rosenau adds that

> traces of norms shared on a global scale can be discerned midst the tensions that are racking local and national communities. The emergence of five of these traces is sufficiently pronounced to warrant singling out as underpinnings of rule systems along the Frontier . . . One is humanitarian issues . . . A second and closely related area is human rights. Another concerns the integrity of democratic institutions, and a fourth involves values pertaining to invasions . . . In a fifth area [is] the environment. (Rosenau 1997, 181-182)

Rosenau (1997, 184) explains that the spread of norms linked to democracy are proven by the number of countries democratized and by the "emergence of norms that justify calling in the 'international community' to observe domestic elections and report on the fairness of their procedures."

Norms as a Body of Theory

Key to understanding international relations is the realization that international interaction is not only a consequence of material conditions, self-interest, or predetermination (Booth and Smith 1995). International relations are also influenced by what Ruggie (1998) calls "ideational causation" and "collective intentionality." There is consensus among various international relations scholars that a norm is a shared understanding of a standard for behavior (Klotz 1995, Finnemore 1996, Ruggie 1998, Finnemore and Sikkink 1998). This definition highlights two key issues about norms. First, a shared understanding is a collective rather than an individual perception. Second, a standard of behavior is a reflection of constitutive rules of behavior.

In the first case, a shared understanding refers to the social nature of reality. A norm exists because of a process of social interaction that encourages inter-subjective understandings, that is, agreements arrived at by a group or collectivity. An inter-subjective understanding is what Ruggie calls a "social fact." Citing John Searle (1995), Ruggie borrows the concept of a social fact to refer to those aspects of reality "produced by virtue of all the relevant actors agreeing that they exist" (Ruggie 1998, 12). Getting to this agreement involves exercising "collective intentionality," that is, expressing cooperative behavior as well as common intent about beliefs, desires, and intentions (Searle 1995, 25). Thus, social facts are created by collective beliefs that agree on the existence of certain practices as facts. Examples of social facts are states, principles in international law, slavery, and other collective international practices, such as democracy promotion. In reference to norms, collectivities and slavery, Allister Sparks notes for example that:

> There is a strange chemistry by which the world from time to time reaches a consensus on some great moral issue. Take the case of slavery. It was practiced for millennia. None of the great religions or great philosophers of antiquity denounced it . . . Then all of a sudden toward the end of the eighteenth century a groundswell of moral concern began to rise in Europe. Slave-owners protested at the time that the system was in accordance with natural law, with God's law . . . To no avail . . . Thus by episodic spasms of concurrence have people gradually expanded their concept of our moral community, the groups of human beings whom it regards as worthy of equal respect

and toward whom one is obligated to behave ethically.
(Sparks 1990)

The importance of addressing the issue of 'social facts,' 'inter-subjective,' or 'shared' understandings in the analysis of norms lies in the fact that some (individual or group based) activities are not exclusively informed by self-interested material circumstances. Actions are often informed or caused by a combination of self-interest, altruism, and collective beliefs. This latest factor was and is a rationale for many kinds of international behavior, including international mobilization over democracy. These kinds of beliefs are not static or permanent, but rather subject to change as new beliefs arrive (such as ending of slavery, formal racial segregation, and colonialism). Most significant is that a social fact remains important in so far as it possesses legitimacy (or collective intentionality), that is, a valid recognition of its existence and relevance among the collective groups who gave it origin. To Held, there is a strong relationship between legitimacy and norms. Legitimacy, he claims (1989, 102), "implies that people follow rules and laws because they think them right, correct, justified–worthy. A legitimate political order is one that is normatively sanctioned by the population."

While the phrase 'shared understanding' refers to the social nature of reality, the idea of a 'standard for behavior' addresses the issue of rules. Standards of behavior are yardsticks or measures stipulating desirable or acceptable forms of social behavior, or what is appropriate and what is not (Kratochwil and Ruggie 1986, 764; Finnemore and Sikkink 1998, 871). In that sense, Hasenclaver, Mayer and Rittberger (1997, 163) explain that norms "embody shared social knowledge, and they have both a regulative and constitutive dimension." That is, norms act as imperatives requiring compliance with standards and help to create a "common social world by fixing the meaning of behavior." This constitutive aspect of a norm defines "the set of practices that make up a particular class of consciously organized social activity–that is to say, they specify what counts as that activity" (Ruggie 1998, 22). To say that norms are constitutive means that a practice only exists because it has received a meaning. Games like chess, for example, are examples of constitutive norms, where the game itself is constituted by its moves. The game defines what counts as the result of a move, such as checkmate. In being constitutive, norms create new (or reshape already existing) categories of activities, interests, or identities; they have an agential function.

Because of social interaction and collective intentionality in international relations, constitutive norms are a mutual development and an important one. They have created the possibility of certain actions arrived at through collective agreement. One of these norms pertains to democracy; the international norm of democratic entitlement says what counts as a democracy and what does not. Thus, international actors adjust their policies to comply with the norm and mobilize to facilitate democracy everywhere. In doing so, the norm shapes actors' identities as well as potentially creating or encouraging the emergence of new actors, such as international civil society groups working on democratization issues. In turn, these groups help to improve and further the norm among states and international organizations.

The Sources of International Norms: Previously Existing Institutions

How do norms come to be? What are the sources of international norms? "How do the normal become normative?" (Raymond 1997, 226). Audie Klotz (1995, 22) answers these questions by explaining that norms do not originate in material interests or coercion, but rather "new norms emerge from within previously existing social institutions." Attaching importance to the origin of a norm as derived from other institutions highlights the presence of an evolutionary process of practices that crystalize in some form of institutionalization (organized or diffuse). Thus, it is important to understand the origin of a norm in an evolutionary context. Moreover, it is important to take into account these various kinds of institutions and their evolutionary make-up.

The gradual process of norm formation and development is contingent on the role played by what Fiorino (1996, 375) refers to as norm entrepreneurs (or norm advocates), individuals or organizations that set out to change the behavior of others. Finnemore and Sikkink (1998) situate these entrepreneurs in an evolutionary norm that develops in three stages. The first stage, norm emergence, is defined as norm entrepreneurs persuading or convincing "a critical mass of relevant states (norm leaders) to embrace new norms" (Finnemore and Sikkink 1998, 895). This stage leads to a threshold point, a situation in which the critical mass of actors adopts the norm, making the transition to the second stage possible. This stage, norm cascading, is the socialization process of a larger number of actors. Third is the internalization of the norm, a stage at which the prescriptions and mechanisms of the norm have all been assimilated and their practice becomes customary.

Two characteristics of the first stage are the efforts of norm entrepreneurs, which take place in a highly contested space involving competition with other norms, and the presence of organizational platforms, which are institutions from which norm entrepreneurs promote or rally for the norm (Finnemore and Sikkink 1998, 898). Sometimes, "the platforms are constructed specifically for the purpose of promoting the norm, as are many nongovernmental organizations (NGOs) (such as Greenpeace, the Red Cross and Transafrica) and the larger transnational advocacy networks of which these NGOs become a part" (Finnemore and Sikkink 1998, 899).

This approach to the origins of norms represents an important cumulative development in the theory of international norms. It acknowledges that, although a norm emerges from previously existing institutions, its implementation or assimilation is gradual and contingent upon the efforts of norm advocates and the ability to socialize others into adopting the values and ideas being promoted. Finnemore and Sikkink assume an inevitable development and acceptance of the norm. In so doing, they fail to acknowledge that circumstance plays a critical role in highlighting the need for the norm and, usually over time, giving advocates the momentum or opportunity to foster it. For example, the norm of decolonization was not merely an effort of notable advocates who decided to support it at the beginning of the century. Opposition to colonization emerged over time and was shaped by people and events. It took the end of the Second World War and the weakening of colonial powers for the norm to gain widespread legitimacy and thus arrive at its momentum.

It is also important to consider the way in which the norm develops. Not all norms evolve uniformly; some have greater success in becoming relevant and being adopted than others. Legro (1997, 34) identifies three factors that influence the strength of a norm: specificity, durability, and concordance. Specificity refers to the clarity of the expected standards of behavior. Some norms are codified in treaties or in declarations; others are customary, and their practice depends on how specific or direct the mandates are. Durability concerns the length of time that the rules have existed, and how critical responses or challenges affect them. To be durable, norms have to develop long-standing legitimacy (Legro 1997, 34). Newly adopted norms are more vulnerable to pressures from various sources, including other norms or practices. The Universal Declaration of Human Rights, for example, adopted in 1948, assumed greater relevance in the 1970s when an increasing number of actors rallied for it, often rejecting the cruder ideological contest between communism and capitalist democracy for the Declaration's universal standards. The norm it represented gained more relevance, in part thanks to its ability to survive the first twenty or more years of the Cold War. Finally, concordance concerns a test of "how widely accepted the rules are in diplomatic discussions and treaties (that is the degree of intersubjective agreement)" (Legro 1997, 35). Although some actors agree to accept and even assimilate the norm, they may qualify their endorsements in different ways. This situation can lead to a lack of agreement between the spirit of the norm and its practice. Dissonance between theory and implementation of a norm depends, however, on whether the norm is constitutive or regulative. When a norm is constitutive, it changes the interests and identities of actors in such a way that it is difficult for the adoptee not to exercise the norm as it has become intrinsic to its identity or being. However, when the norm lacks constitutive feature and is only regulative, it invites or encourages a kind of behavior without necessarily requiring an actor to change. The actor may choose to adopt the norm with greater reservations.

In addition to Legro's three factors, two additional characteristics that require attention are continuity and audience. Even norms that are adopted and reach the threshold point in the first stage can remain dormant in the second stage. New norms may appear, new or contesting ideas or interests may interrupt the adoption of the norm, or the norm may take a different direction. Norm discontinuity diminishes the strength of the norm and makes it harder for actors to popularize it. Some features of the norm of democracy remained dormant for a long period of time during the Cold War years.

The norm's audience also determines its strength. Norm advocates need to identify and reach out to audiences, foreign and domestic, that are in a condition to listen to the message or be mobilized. Again, the circumstance of the moment is critical for the adoption of the emerging norm. The audience is no longer only the nation-state; because of increased global interconnectedness, states are but one key set of actors among others with international or intermestic concerns. Citizens, NGOs (international or local), and international organizations are also audiences of norm entrepreneurs.

In summary, the development of these stages depends on the advocates and circumstances facilitating the emergence of the norm. The socialization of these values is contingent upon the strategies adopted by the advocates as well as by the clarity of the mandates and the continuity of practices. Ultimately the internalization of the norm will depend on its durability as well as on the extent to which practices conform to the norm. Whenever there is a gap between theory (norm) and practice, activists or norm advocates are stimulated to urge for norm compliance.

The impact of norms The effect of the norm on the actor is an important feature and is contingent to it being assimilated. A norm impacts an actor who adopts it. That is, adopting the norm changes the interest and identity of an actor; a norm's initial impact is observed in that change. For example, when England fully adopted the norm of decolonization, it changed its policy with regards to other territories or lands in its empire and endorsed the principle of self-determination. The impact of the norm on an actor's behavior is observed in the various ways the actor can exercise the norm. Actors who follow the norm intend to change certain aspects of reality. Looking at what the actors do in the world is an important reflection of the extent to which the norm is exercised. Thus, three effects of the norm are observed, the change in interest and identity that occurs from adopting the norm, the various ways the norm is exercised, and the effect the actor has on the world when acting according to the new norm.

International Support for Democracy

As noted, Klotz (1995, 22-23) emphasizes that norms emerge from preexisting institutional structures, such as those promoting liberal individualism and sovereignty. She argues that actors are already embedded in these institutions and use this position to constitute new interests and identities that reinforce and legitimize the practice of norms. In this context, a norm about democracy embedded in previously existing institutions informs groups to invoke international mobilization or advocacy to promote democracy where it is absent. It highlights the importance of democracy as the legitimate form of government and the need for its universal adoption. This claim is tangibly expressed in struggles by countries and other international actors to make democracy global. As Harris and Reilly (1998, 368) stress, "since the late 1980s, the international community has introduced a normative and political dimension to development cooperation policy and introduced new criteria for aid and foreign policy with good governance and democracy as core objectives."

Groups and individuals share a normative commitment that their moral and political responsibilities about freedom and equality, and rule by the people, do not only reside within the boundaries of sovereign states, but rather are inclusive of any social, political, or economic constructs. In other words, international mobilization is explained by an emerging norm of democratic support that claims that rule by the people is a universal human right rooted in the principle of individual and group sovereignty and liberal values, and that it is a responsibility of all to ensure the success of democracy.

Thomas Franck (1995, 84) has argued that the international community is increasingly requiring governments to recognize that "as a prerequisite to membership of the community of nations, [they must] derive 'their just powers from the consent of the governed.'" This normative requirement "is finding its way into codes of regional and global standards and into the practice and jurisprudence of international institutions" (Franck 1995, 85). In fact, in 1991 at the forty-fifth session of the General Assembly of the UN, the members adopted a key resolution that has marked the transition point to accepting the norm of democracy in international politics and law, thereby extending the international responsibilities of its members. The resolution, entitled

Enhancing the Effectiveness of the Principle of Periodic and Genuine Elections, stresses that:

> Periodic and genuine elections are a necessary and indispensable element of sustained efforts to protect the rights and interests of the governed and that, as a matter of practical experience, the right of everyone to take part in the government of his or her country is a crucial factor in the effective enjoyment by all of a wide range of other human rights and fundamental freedoms, embracing political, economic, social and cultural rights. (UN General Assembly Resolution 45/150, February 21, 1991)

This is an emerging norm in its early stage of socialization that, while not internalized, has influenced the behavior of the international community.

The Role of Previously Existing Institutions

Franck (1995, 91) argues that one can think of democratic entitlement, the conception that every nation is entitled to be democratic, as three generational, that is, based on three previously existing normative institutions: self-determination (or sovereignty), freedom of expression, and electoral rights. In his view, "these three subsets expound the right to free civil association, the right to political discourse, and the right to vote." Each one of these institutions are early precursors of the idea of the validity of democracy and its support on a world wide scale.

Self-determination was an early precursor to the norm of democratic entitlement and provided a standard to follow for international actors. Self-determination has to do with the collective right of a people to govern themselves, creating a voluntary civil society usually by means of a state in secession from a prior affiliation (Franck 1995, 92). As self-determination evolved in practice and rhetoric it took different "shapes with different contexts as it was transported over time and space and empowered in different circumstances" (Jackson 1993, 119). Self-determination evolved from a stated principle to a right and has remained linked to democracy. This will of a body of people who define themselves as an entity not only refers to a process – independence from outside forces but also contains an internal aspect: democracy. Hannum emphasizes that "this internal aspect, the conviction that the only legitimate basis for government is the consent of the governed, provided the ultimate justification for decolonization" (Hannum 1996, 973). Goertz (1994, 251) argues that the principle of self-determination embodied in the norm of decolonization "flowed naturally out of the continued struggle in Europe to extend democracy to more than wealthy white males: if women should have a say in their governments, why not Africans?"

Self-determination evolved in various stages from the American and French Revolution in 1776 and 1789, respectively, to pro-independence movements in Hispanic America in the nineteenth century advocating "peoples rather than princes (or dynasties) as the only valid grounds for international legitimacy: [that is] national self-determination" (Jackson 1993, 120). The norm later evolved into the European consultations for self-determination influenced by Woodrow Wilson and was applied to some of the defeated countries and disintegrating empires after World War I. After the end of World War II, self-determination gained further impetus with growing nationalist movements in the developing world. With the emergence of the United Nations, increasing numbers of resolutions called for measures that would ensure the right of peoples and nations to self determination. The UN concluded in 1960 that "all peoples have the right to self-determination." By 1980, most former colonizers had yielded to independence territories they once claimed.

A key feature in the decolonization process was the UN's role in setting normative standards and carrying out elections and referendums in many colonies seeking independence. As the struggles for colonial independence decreased, the issue of self-determination shifted its focus to its internal dimension: human rights protection and democracy. Human rights issues grew in relevance in the 1970s and 1980s, and international attention became more receptive to these problems.

Human rights are entitlements bestowed to (and by) all individuals regardless of race, gender, age, or other social status. These entitlements empower and ensure people of the inalienability of their lives, as well as their social conditions as free and equal beings. Like self-determination, human rights emerged from the ideas and movements of the French and American Revolutions that claimed liberty, equality, and solidarity among all individuals. The most important human rights instruments available to the international community took shape in the twentieth century after World War II: the Universal Declaration of Human Rights (UDHR), enacted in 1948, and the Covenant on Civil and Political Rights (CCPR), enacted twenty years later.

Human rights and democracy have shared a historic link since the incidence of the former. First, democracy, understood as rule by the people, has been contingent on the presence of at least two prerequisites: unconstrained freedom of association for individuals to manifest their preferences about public goods and government, and the opportunity to freely express and deliberate about one's ideas and preferences about public matters. Both the

Universal Declaration of Human Rights and the Covenant on Civil and Political Rights transformed these ideas into rights. Second, the notion of representation through election as a key component of contemporary democracy was also composed by these human rights instruments and later served as a basis for normative action.

Self-determination and human rights have been intimately connected in the historic experiences of societies that pursue independence and freedom. Democracy has also maintained a strong linkage between these two rights. However, democracy has been recognized as a claim in its own right by individuals and groups. The right to political participation is an entitlement recognized by the international community and reflected in international norms as "the right to take part in the conduct of public affairs or government, and the relatively specific right to vote in elections" (Steiner 1996, 661-662). The two key international rights documents, the Universal Declaration and the Covenant, make participation in politics a right of everyone. Article 21 of the Universal Declaration establishes that

> (1) Everyone has the right to take part in the government of his country directly through freely chosen representatives. . .(3) The will of the people shall be the basis of the authority of government; this will shall be expressed in periodic and genuine elections which shall be by universal and equal suffrage and shall be held by secret vote or by equivalent voting procedures.

This declaration had an important impact on the international community. It later led to the passing, in 1966, of the Covenant on Civil and Political Rights, the first legal instrument to identitfy democracy as a right Article 25 stressed that every citizen has a right to freely choose a representative or to take part in the conduct of public affairs. It also asserted that people have the right to vote in elections (CCPR).[3]

Franck (1995, 100) stresses that the Covenant marked a shift or orientation in thinking about rights:

> It established discursive rights of political participation, pioneered in connection with colonies and now made

---

[3] The covenant stipulated that citizens have the right "(a) To take part in the conduct of public affairs, directly or through freely chosen representatives; (b) To vote and to be elected at genuine periodic elections which shall be by universal and equal suffrage and shall be held by secret ballot, guaranteeing the free expression of the will of the electors;"

universally applicable by the Covenant. It shifted prior focus from 'peoples' to persons, from decolonization to personal political participatory entitlements in independent nations. It entitles persons in all states to free, fair, and open participation in the democratic process of governance chosen by each state.

The normative components did not remain in the discursive realm. The UN created the Human Rights Committee, whose function consisted of investigating the status of civil and political rights and "the progress made in the enjoyment of those rights." Moreover, regional bodies also adopted specific norms with regards to human rights and democracy.

International Democracy Advocates and Changing Conditions

These norms associated with democracy influenced and informed a post-Second World War democracy movement that has evolved from seeking recognition of democracy as the legitimate form of government, to its support on a worldwide basis to an institutionalization through various practices in expanding and consolidating democracy beyond a minimum standard.

In the first half of the twentieth century democracy was still a new experiment; until then very few regimes exhibited democratic features. Fox (1992, 249) reminds readers that universal suffrage in independent countries was still a new phenomenon: "women, for example, became entitled to vote on equal standing with men in the Netherlands only in 1919, the United Kingdom in 1928, Spain in 1931, France in 1944, Greece in 1956 and Portugal in 1968." The rights of people of color are another indicator of democracy or the lack thereof. In the United States, poll taxes that prevented blacks from voting were only outlawed in the 1960s. When the Organization of the United Nations was created in 1945, only a handful of countries exhibited some feature of being democratic.

The widespread recognition of democracy began during the World War II with the Allies' claim that the war was a fight for democracy. By 1948, democracy was recognized in the UDHR, later reenforced in 1966 by the CCPR and its subsequent addendums as the legitimate form of government. However, the relatively new support for democracy was constrained during the second half of the twentieth century by two major global events: the Cold War and decolonization.

The Cold War was the strategic and political struggle that originated after World War II between the United States and its Western European allies, on one hand, and the USSR and Communist countries, on the other. This confrontation created an ideological divide between socialist and capitalist camps that competed for spheres of influence, and economic, territorial and military control. The Soviet Union and other socialist countries tended to dismiss democracy as a construction of anti-communism or bourgeois politics. In contrast, anti-communism was equivalent to democracy to the United States. This simplistic formulation led to U.S. support for anti-democratic governments and actions in the name of ideological superiority.

Amidst these engagements, struggles for decolonization assumed a high priority on the international agenda. After World War II and with the creation of the United Nations, world politics focused on recovering from the war and maintaining peace and stability by upholding the rights of nations through the norms of equal sovereignty and non-intervention. The claim of sovereignty attracted international attention due to the lack of sovereignty in colonized territories.

These colonies were mostly successful in achieving political independence, predominantly from 1945 to 1980. However, although the transfer of power to new national elites was widespread, democratization did not always follow or last. Fred Haliday (1989, 27-28) highlights three processes that accompanied, or followed, the struggles for self-determination from colonial rule. First, nationalist movements in Africa and Asia combined their struggles with social revolutionary agendas.[4] These agendas involved economic strategies associated with socialist goals that gave greater preference to economic equality than free choice. Second, Haliday points out that, as independence was achieved, boundary and territorial wars between third world countries followed. Examples of these conflicts were the Arab-Israeli wars, the Indo-Pakistani conflicts, and the wars in the Horn of Africa. Third, the East-West conflict involved newly independent countries in the Cold War confrontations between Western democracies and the Soviet Union as independence movements and new countries were pressured to take sides and forge alliances with the dominant powers.

One key consequence of these three processes was the inability to forge democratic regimes. From the post-independence periods, many countries fell into some kind of dictatorship that restricted civil and political liberties and exacerbated social inequality. With regards to Africa, Kaballo (1995, 192)

---

[4] In Latin America, most guerrilla movements similarly included nationalist and revolutionary components. Their nationalism, though different from anti-colonial movements, claimed to be anti-imperialist (anti-US), and against neo-colonialism. Movements like those of Nicaraguan, Salvadoran and Colombian groups illustrate this point. These groups labeled themselves as national liberation movements. For example, Frente Farabundo Marti para la Liberacion Nacional for El Salvador, Frente Sandinista de Liberacion Nacional (in Nicargua), and Ejercito de Liberacion Nacional (Colombia). (Castaneda, 1994).

explains that the history of these countries "since independence has been one of collapse into authoritarian rule," caused either by military coup d'etat or civilian coups perpetrated by a ruling party, thus hampering the chances of multiparty governments. Prior to the end of the Cold War most developing countries were experiencing some form of non-democratic rule (manifested by military or one-party rule) which in some cases included widespread state-sponsored violence (ranging from killings and disappearances to imprisonment and exile), and internal war. Table 3.1 shows that between 1945 and 1994 there were nearly two hundred wars, most of them taking place in the third world. The table also shows that two-thirds of these conflicts were of an internal nature. Nearly half of these conflicts occurred before 1970 (Licklider 1995).

Table 3.1 Wars by Region and Type, 1945-1994

Region	(%)	Types of War	N	(%)
South and South East Asia	25.27%	Anti-regime wars	58	31.18%
Sub Saharan Africa	20.97%	Wars of secession	44	23.66%
East Asia	3.76%	Hybrid wars	21	11.29%
Central America/Caribbean	8.60%	International wars	30	16.13%
Middle East	22.58%	Decolonization wars	11	5.91%
Europe	6.45%	Other	22	11.83%
North Africa	4.84%	*Total*	186	100
South America	7.53%			

Source: Haushler and Kennedy 1994, 178-181.

This context gave rise to an emphasis on human rights and renewed struggles for democracy. These efforts, however, had to fight against the principle of non-intervention and international economic injustice. Newly independent countries (and even those belonging to the inter-American system) argued that sovereignty was unconditional and inviolable. They asserted the right to political independence, by which no other state could exert influence on their sovereign form of government. Furthermore, in addition to upholding the right of non-intervention, the post-World War II period saw the emergence of an economic order that introduced new mechanisms of international trade and investment but kept the historic links forged by colonial rule, thus leaving developing countries at an economic disadvantage. The emerging developing world called for greater international economic fairness, especially with regard to unequal terms of trade. Such demands remain unresolved. Despite these multiple setbacks for democracy, efforts to support democracy continued. The struggles to support democracy emanated in large part from struggles to protect human rights and gained relevance in the 1980s.

The international norm of democracy had been included in the instruments established by the Universal Declaration and the Covenant. The norm stipulated the right to participate in the political process via universal suffrage. Subsequent developments in the 1970s in various regional bodies, such as the Inter-American Human Rights Commission, the European Court on Human Rights and the African Commission on Human and People's Rights helped to safeguard democracy as a normative concern. Most important was the work of a growing network of activists and movements advocating human rights and democracy.

The efforts of local activists and international organizations advocating protection of human rights in various parts of the world led to the establishment of transnational networks of support and cooperation that further internationalized the life of non-democratic nation-states by exposing practices that went against international human rights and democratic norms Networking was established between local leaders (churches, social movements, human rights organizations, notable personalities, political leaders, etc.) and various kinds of international actors (international organizations, international civil society, states) as a response to strengthening principles and identifying abuses. There was an interaction between principled beliefs, advocacy, and conditions in various parts of the world. Circumstances, thus, played a major role in providing the opportunity to act.

In Latin America, human rights networks worked together closely to publicize abuses, as well as in seeking investigations about why and how people were killed, disappeared, or imprisoned and who the victims and perpetrators were (Clark 2001). Demands for improved treatment and respect for the lives of activists and other leaders in Southern Cone countries and Central America were made under the banners of human rights and democracy promotion. This process was facilitated in part by the work of regional bodies. The Inter-American Human Rights Court, for example, investigated abuses, followed events, and ruled in cases of rights abuses in the region during the 1970s and thereafter. In African countries, where a large number of civil wars took place, various organizations advocated measures such as safe havens for refugees or an end to targeted killings.

An especially important illustration of transnational advocacy and norm compliance is the development of human rights groups after the signing of the Helsinki accords in 1975. The implementation of these accords helped create and revive human rights groups in Eastern Europe. The Helsinki Conference, started in 1973, was a result of cooperation between the East and the West aimed at legitimizing the division of Europe following the end of World War II (Burgenthal 1992, 256). Although the accord dealt primarily with security issues, it included a human rights component. William Korey explains that, because the USSR was concerned in particular with international recognition of the division of the two Germanies, "it had to accept positive– even if limited–developments in human rights as expressed in Principle 7 [of the Act]" (Korey 1998, 231). Principle 7 of the Helsinki Act, to which the Soviet Union became a signatory, stipulated "respect for human rights and freedoms." The implementation of the Helsinki agreement in Eastern Europe gave origin to the creation of the Moscow-based Helsinki Watch Group formed by dissidents from various sectors of Soviet society. The Watch Group later helped to create or inspire similar movements in other parts of Eastern Europe. In Poland the Committee of Workers Defense (KOR), later renamed Solidarity, and in Czechoslovakia the Chapter 77 movement, formed in early 1977 after learning of the efforts of the Watch Group at international human rights conferences.

It is important to add that in the context of international law, the 1970s were also the decade in which the Covenant of Civil and Political Rights entered into force. One key element of its development was the creation of the Human Rights Committee, whose work consisted of reporting on country conditions and examining rights cases. This situation motivated activists to demand that the UN play a role in rights protection and increase monitoring of compliance with the Covenant. As Korey points out, the power of the Committee has grown significantly over the years (Korey 1998, 267).

The emergence of the human rights norm depended not only on the skills and abilities of norm advocates and their platforms, but also on the circumstances that provided the opportunity to act. These networks originally focused on the protection of lives or freedoms of individuals. As the work of these organizations continued, however, a link between human rights and democracy was emphasized: human rights issues were brought to public attention and were linked to the absence of democracy. In Southern Cone countries, efforts to end restrictions on civil liberties led to the political liberalization process. But once liberalization was set in motion, activists continued pressing for democratization. This process was also encouraged gradually through the legal instruments enacted by the OAS. Following the adoption of the Covenant on Civil and Political Rights, in 1969 the OAS passed the American Convention on Human Rights. This accord provides for the right of political participation by citizens of a country, "to vote and to be elected in genuine periodic elections, which shall be by universal and equal suffrage and by secret by ballot that guarantees the free expression of the will of the voters" (Padilla and Houpert 1997, 82). As well as establishing democratic norms at an international level, the Convention served as a basis for requests for rights compliance by the Inter-American Human Rights Court. As human rights and democracy were linked, so were democracy and peace.

Peace workers and other activists established the link between security and democracy in an attempt to end warfare. A link between internal conflict and undemocratic conditions was made, establishing that democratic systems have positive effects in forging enduring settlements to civil wars. Harris and Reilly (1998, 17) point out that democracies

> have a degree of legitimacy, inclusiveness, flexibility and capacity for constant adaptation that enables deep rooted conflict to be managed peacefully. Moreover, by building norms of behavior of negotiation, compromise, and cooperation amongst political actors, democracy itself has a pacifying effect on the nature of political relations between people and between governments.

The efforts of rights advocates in transnational networks increased the exposure of nation-states to international scrutiny. By internationalizing human rights violations and instruments, the denial of individuals' rights in one country become the concern of other nations. Orentlicher (1992, 340) notes that countries are expected to react to other countries' abuses of fundamental rights; indeed, "the whole point of making human rights the subject of international law is to assure universal enjoyment of those rights by establishing international accountability for their violations."

A key issue of international activism and advocacy is that norm advocates have reconciled an apparent contradiction between non-intervention and international protection of human rights and democracy. They showed that, in practice, sovereignty in non-democracies was questionable or suspect, not because of external threats, but because the denial of democracy and rights by dictatorships and wars undermined or eviscerated the political community, the people in whom sovereignty resides.

International efforts on behalf of human rights and peace gradually expanded in the 1980s into support for democratization. Party internationals, NGOs, leaders, states, and international organizations increased their international pressures on undemocratic societies to comply with democratic norms, like the denial of political rights specifically fair and free universal suffrage. This insistence gave birth to a number of new organizations that emerged from both democracies and undemocratic countries, as well as from local opposition groups and their networking activities. These groups often existed across borders, and so came to establish and extend the realm of international civil society. The Human Rights Law Group, the National Endowment for Democracy, the International Parliamentary Union, the Carter Center, the International Institute for Democracy and Electoral Assistance (IDEA), the International Foundation for Election Systems (IFES), the National Democratic Institute and the National Republican Institute, for example, are all organizations that were internationalized in the early 1980s in response to demands for democratization. In most cases the emphasis paid by these groups was the call for eliminating fraudulent elections and allowing opposition groups to form and rally without coercion and intimidation.

In addition to these organizations, a wide range of more than fifty foundations committed to support democracy abroad. Examples range from the Carnegie Foundations and the Open Society Institute to the Ford, Mellon, Arias and Soros Foundations (Quigley 1997). Transnational networking and emerging organizations continue to expose non-democratic practices as violating international standards. In this way, they help to give continuity to the norm, ensuring its durability.

These various factors contributed to a gradual acceptance of the norm in the international community. As Wippman (1997, 667) stresses with reference to elections as one of the norms for political participation, by the end of the 1980s and early 1990s there was "relatively broad (though by no means uniform) acceptance of the principle that elections should entail competition among multiple political parties. . . Additionally, substantial international agreement now exists on many of the procedural and substantive prerequisites for free and fair elections."

The universal adoption of the norm is also reflected in the establishment of electoral assistance functions by the United Nations at the request of its members, who seek external legitimation for its international and domestic efforts. Rosenau identifies these election monitoring efforts "not simply [as] instances of local political systems choosing their leaderships; they are also instances of global politics, of the international community crossing sovereign boundaries to participate in the internal affairs of states" (Rosenau 1997, 256). Electoral monitoring reflects at least three tendencies: a shared recognition that free and fair elections are a key element of democracy and political participation; that states seek legitimacy and recognition of their regimes through external electoral monitoring; and that there is a growing internalization of globalization in the domestic political life of states. Thus, states and non-state actors continue to support democracy abroad.

European countries, for example, have influenced and been influenced by international norms of democracy. Their influence emerges from work within the regional body, the European Union, and from wider international developments. Sweden and Germany are examples of countries whose foreign policies have changed due to normative influences. Germany has incorporated democracy promotion as a key element in its foreign policy and assistance programs. It has done so particularly in its work within the European Union as well as in its support to various German organizations and foundations working on democracy abroad.

Sweden, also has informed and been affected by international democratization. The Swedish International Development Agency (SIDA) instituted a section on democracy, the Department of Democracy and Social Development. In 1997, it established a division for democratic governance. SIDA considers that the fulfilment of certain minimum requirements is necessary for democracy. These essential features include "free elections of alternative representatives, an independent legal system and fundamental democratic rights and privileges. Equality between women and men is both a question of human rights and a prerequisite for sustainable development" (SIDA 1999). The U.S. changed its foreign policy with regards to democracy.

The U.S. also adapted its foreign policy with regards to democracy. Recent foreign policy changes reflect the influence of globalization in strengthening international norms of democracy. In 1990, AID underwent an historic development as its mission and mandate changed with the introduction of its "Democratic Initiative." The initiative established the promotion of democracy as a central aim of AID and it represented a consensus arrived at among the foreign policy establishment. The consensus, notes Wiarda (1997, 16) consisted of three related goals "(1) *democracy* (mainly meaning elections) and human rights; (2) *open markets*–coupled with privatization, state-downsizing; and (3) *free trade*, within a larger common-market arrangement." However, AID strategy has expanded its mandate of democracy to far reaching goals extending its work beyond elections and human rights. In 1997, AID set four objectives for its democracy program: "a) rule of law and respect for human rights strengthened; b) credible and competitive political processes encouraged; c) development of a politically active civil society promoted; and d) transparent and accountable government institutions encouraged" (USAID 1998). These goals reflect the changing international environment as well as the normative influence that has gradually extended demands for political participation beyond the electoral scenario. This latter point has been of particular consequence for the internationalization of civil society, which stresses the need for more citizen freedom and involvement in political processes.

Regional bodies like the European Union and the Organization of American States have been crucial in the establishment of norm compliance, particularly in the process of socialization and internalization. Building from the Universal Declaration of Human Rights, the European Union adheres to its preference for democracy and human rights. Moreover, the European Union declares that its justification for mobilizing abroad on behalf of democracy is rooted in that declaration: "European Union action is grounded in the general framework of the United Nations Charter and the Universal Declaration of Human Rights, supplemented by the two international covenants of 1966 on civil and political rights and economic, social and cultural rights." The European Union not only stresses that involvement is justified by these international norms, but that these norms identify the principle of non-intervention as a relative one: "human rights are an important legitimate aspect of relations between States and no State can invoke the principle of non-interference as grounds for rejecting any manifestation of concern by other States at human rights violations" (European Union 1998).

The OAS highlights similar issues to those of the European Union. This institution has demonstrated a historic commitment to democracy. This concern was most recently translated into the creation of the Unit for the Promotion of Democracy (UPD) in 1990. The endorsement of democracy in the Inter-American system is not a new phenomenon, indeed, there is a long tradition behind it. The 1936 Declaration of Principles of Inter-American Solidarity and Cooperation is perhaps the earliest recognition in the twentieth century of the importance of common democracy throughout the Americas (Acevedo and Grossman 1996). After the OAS was created, the American Declaration of the Rights and Duties of Man included support for political participation of all citizens in the hemisphere. This belief was later endorsed in the 1959 Santiago Declaration shortly after Fidel Castro overthrew the Cuban dictator, Fulgencio Batista. The Cold War period reoriented the commitment to democracy toward anti-communism, but equally important is that the principled desire for democracy was traditionally in competition with a stronger norm, that of security. In particular, the OAS has been committed to the principle of non-intervention. During the authoritarian period in Latin American countries in the Cold War years, this argument was used to thwart collective democratization efforts.

The commitment of various democratic countries, the work of NGOs, and the continued work of the Inter-American Commission on Human Rights and the Inter-American Human Rights Court influenced the OAS to renew its commitment to democracy. In fact, as the region becomes more democratic, the OAS gives greater endorsement to the norm of democracy. In 1985, following the substantial decline in military rule, the OAS amended its charter through the Protocol of Cartagena de Indias to declare that "representative democracy is an indispensable condition for the stability, peace and development of the region." But it was Resolution 1080 that fundamentally shifted the OAS's commitment toward democracy (Lutz 1997, 649). OAS members created a procedure to convene foreign ministers in the event of a coup d'etat, therefore allowing the institution to collectively defend democracy. This procedure was intended to bolster the work of the UPD.

The efforts to strengthen democracy in the hemisphere did not end with Resolution 1080. After the third Summit of the Americas in March 2001, the members of the OAS proposed the establishment of a Democratic Charter. The Charter was adopted in September of that year by all member states and defined in its article 3 what constituted a democracy among members of the OAS and what were the key binding attributes of a democracy among the members of the Inter-American System. The Article 8 of the chart established that "Member states reaffirm their intention to strengthen the inter-American system for the protection of human rights for the consolidation of democracy in the Hemisphere." The Chart also stipulates that "any unconstitutional alteration or interruption of the democratic order in a state of the Hemisphere constitutes an insurmountable obstacle to the participation of that state's government in the Summits of the Americas process." Moreover, Article 20 of the Chart declared that upon determination by the OAS that a country had interrupted its democratic order, the Organization could "suspend said member state from the exercise of its right to participate in the OAS" (Inter-American Democratic Charter 2001).

As the commitment to democracy has increased, so have the number of institutions and organizations working for democracy both directly and indirectly. This trend further increases the number of democratic norm advocates. In February 1999, for example, The "World Movement for Democracy" was launched in New Delhi, India, by democracy advocates from more than 80 countries. In its founding statement, the members stressed that the "goal of building a worldwide movement for democracy presupposes the universality of the democratic idea." It also expressed a commitment to consolidate democratic gains, and promote democratic transitions, as well as to develop world movement networks (Founding Statement 1999).

These advocates tend to have a broad view of what democracy promotion and entrenchment entails. There has therefore also been a gradual shift "away from the specific events surrounding election day to the consolidation of institutions and processes which are essential to viable democracies" (UN A/52/474 Resolution, 16 October 1997). The end result has been a process of democratic expansion influenced by a normative commitment translated in what Carothers (1999, 85) denominates as core strategies that "incorporate both a model of democracy and a model of democratization," namely, elections, state institutions and civil society. A look at Figure 3.1 shows the electoral assistance functions provided by the United Nations which suggests an increase in the early 1990s and then a gradual decline. Joyner (1999) has argued that the decline may be "attributable to democratic electoral systems taking root in many of these emerging civil societies, with less need for U.N. support" (347). Two other explanations to this decline can be offered. First, as the UN expressed it, there has been a shift away from electoral support to other political institutions. Second, the functions of supporting electoral work has been expanded to a wider array of international actors other than the UN.

One sphere in which the shift in supporting other political institutions is observed is in the development of international conferences on democracy and democratization. International conferences play a key role as mechanisms to advance norms in support of democracy. Global conferences have made significant impacts in the international community by mobilizing national and local governments, non-governmental organizations (NGOs) to take action on a major global problem. Conferences have been important in "establishing international standards and guidelines for national policy; serving as a forum where new proposals can be debated and consensus sought; setting in motion a process, whereby governments make commitments and report back regularly to the United Nations" (UN 1997).

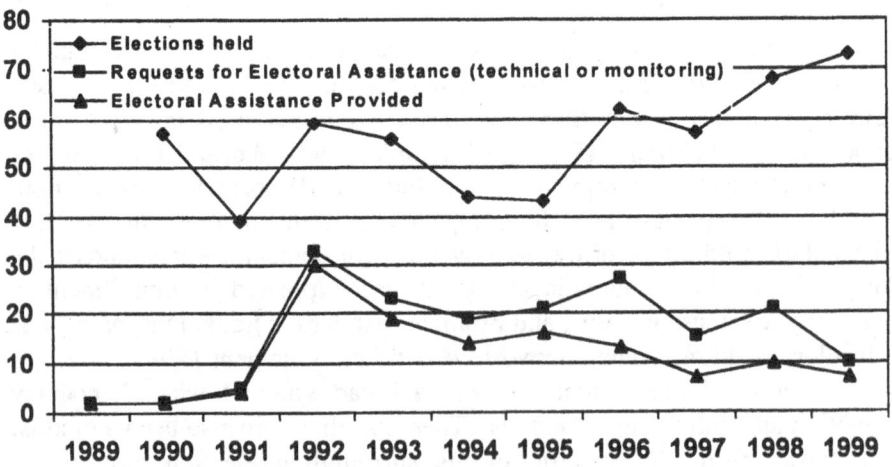

Figure 3.1 Worldwide Elections and UN Assistance

The most important democracy related conferences are: The UN Conference on New and Restored Democracies, with four conferences now: Manila, Philippines, 1988; Managua, Nicaragua, 1994, Bucharest, Romania, September 1997, and Benin 2000. Another event is that of the World Movement for Democracy which had held two conferences one in February 1999 in India, and another on November 2000 in Brazil. Finally, the World Forum on Democracy which started last year and is sponsoring the Community of Democracies Initiative inaugurated in July of 2000. Table below shows the different major conferences on Democracy that have been held in the past ten years.

Table 3.2 Global Conferences on Democracy

Date and Place	Issues addressed
UN Conference on New and Restored Democracies	
Manila, Philippines, June, 1988	Manila Declaration: Reaffirms link between peace, democracy and development
Managua, Nicaragua, July, 1994	Plan of action: Promoting acceptance of and respect for democratic principles
Bucharest, Romania, September 1997	Guidelines for strengthening policies and principles addressed to the governments of the new or restored democracies
Cotonou, Benin, December, 2000	Peace, Security, Democracy and Development
World Movement for Democracy	
New Dehli, India, February, 1999	Founding Statement: outlines the purposes and aims of this [World Movement for Democracy] "pro-active network of democrats."
Sao Paolo, Brazil, November, 2000	• Presentation of "Democracy Courage Tributes":
World Forum on Democracy	
Warsaw, Poland, June, 2000	Appeal to endorse and establish a caucus of democracies at the United Nations.

Chapter 4

The International Political Context of Nicaragua: from U.S. Intervention to International Involvement

International mobilization to promote democracy in Nicaragua is linked to a particular set of historical and political relationships that began with undemocratic U.S. influence in domestic politics and more recently involves active international support for democratization. The 1979 Nicaraguan Revolution that overthrew the Somoza dictatorship established a new pattern of international relations for Nicaragua that changed the terms of the country's traditional dependence on the United States. This change allowed a range of new international actors to participate in the building of Nicaragua after Somoza. As the country's political crisis deepened in the mid to late 1980s, international actors influenced local leaders to negotiate and hold open elections. With the first free elections and the political opening in the country, international actors participated in the democratization of the country in more sustained manner.

Nicaragua pre-1979

Nicaragua has been dependent as a state since its independence in 1821. The country's initial dependence resulted from international market relations in which Nicaragua relied on indigo and coffee exports until the late nineteenth-century. Then, persistent U.S. military intervention led to the consolidation of dependence at all levels; economic, social, cultural, and political. Foreign military intervention in Nicaragua created a dependent state with an incipient organizational structure to serve the interests of the United States, which forged a power alliance between foreign capital, largely of American origin, and certain local elites. This alliance led to the creation of the Nicaraguan National Guard and a number of institutions that coordinated the economic activities of mainly U.S.-owned companies in Nicaragua. In practical terms, while Nicaragua maintained its official status of a sovereign republic, "the direct intervention of the foreign power [the United States] in Nicaragua in the political arena had the main effect of dissolving the national State" (Velasquez Pereira 1992, 146).

The dictatorship and dynastic regimes of the Somoza family, which were a direct creation of the United States forces in Nicaragua, followed the same stands as the U.S. and received full support from that country. Domestically, the dictatorship allowed foreign capital to penetrate the national economy. Somoza secured a tight and repressive regime which was supplied by U.S. military aid and U.S. foreign military sales. For this reason, any resistance movement organized against the Somoza dictatorship would also oppose the government that created and supported the dictatorship, namely the United States. The Sandinista movement (the Sandinista National Liberation Front), which became the architect of the Nicaraguan revolution, had made clear that the overthrow of Somoza implied a break with the prevalence of U.S. interests over national ones.

The 1979-1989 Nicaraguan Revolution and its International Context

The Nicaraguan revolution represented a historical rupture from U.S. intervention and affected all the countries of Central America, the U.S., and other international actors who had traditionally been less involved in Nicaragua. Three parallel patterns developed in the revolutionary process. While tensions with the U.S. substantially heightened, new international actors became involved in the country's political process, and some actors already started to show signs of promoting democratization in the country.

The fall of Somoza represented a direct defeat for American policy, a situation that under the Reagan administration led to growing anti-Sandinismo. Such antagonism was reflected in a U.S. embargo and support for a counterrevolutionary movement organized by former members of Somoza's National Guard, known as contras. Support for the contras as well as the economic embargo turned the conflict into a civil war with international dimensions that complicated the crisis and delayed a negotiated settlement.

In fact, while tensions with the United States grew, the Nicaraguan revolution became an opportunity for other international actors to participate and assist in the reconstruction of the country's economic and political structures. Although this was not the first time that international actors were involved in Nicaraguan politics, the international community had overwhelmingly, if not rhetorically or diplomatically, supported the struggle against Somoza, international solidarity was manifest in the support of the few Latin American democracies, Canada, Western Europe, social movements that organized committees of solidarity with the people of Nicaragua, and other actors such as European NGOs. At the same time, Cuba, Eastern Europe and the former Soviet Union became actively involved in Nicaraguan politics.

As part of a policy of diversifying relations with the rest of the world (Van der Laan 1986), the Sandinista government invited international actors to come to Nicaragua and support the revolution through aid, material support, and technical cooperation. The Soviet Union, East Germany, Bulgaria, Hungary, and Czechoslovakia, for example, were major partners of the Sandinistas. In fact, in addition to U.S. antagonism towards the Sandinistas, involvement of Eastern bloc countries in Nicaraguan issues became a crucial variable in turning the internal conflict into one of international dimensions. While estimates of the value of military assistance cannot always be confirmed, economic aid to Nicaragua by Eastern European countries totaled nearly six billion dollars during the 1980s. Table 4.1 shows the flow of Eastern European and Soviet economic aid to Nicaragua during the revolution. As the table shows, the flow of aid increased substantially during the mid-eighties. Three quarters of the assistance was in the form of loans (INICAE 1991, 157).

Table 4.1 Foreign Aid by Socialist Countries to Nicaragua, 1979-1989

	Comecon*	Other	Total
1979 to 1980	133.2	--	133.2
1981-1985	2688.8	71.6	2760.4
1986 to 1989	1731.8	--	1731.8
	4553.8	71.6	4625.4

Source: INICAE 1991, 157. Figures are in millions of dollars.*CMEA, Council for Mutual Economic Assistance (members included: USSR, Bulgaria, Czechoslovakia, Hungary, Poland, Romania, East Germany, Cuba, Mongolia and Vietnam).

In addition to Eastern European involvement in Nicaragua, Scandinavian countries became interested in helping the country economically. As Table 4.2 shows, in the 1980s Norway, Sweden, and the Netherlands provided double the official development assistance of France, Germany, Italy, and England combined, although these countries had enjoyed a longer relationship with Central America. Moreover, these international newcomers focused more on development projects than in financing balance of payments deficits (Orozco 1995a).

Table 4.2 Official Development Assistance to Nicaragua, 1980-1989

	1980 to 1983	1984 to 1986	1987 to 1989	
Canada	23.8	27.8	14.5	66.1
France	33.2	40.6	14.3	88.1
Germany	49.3	23.2	19.6	92.1
Italy	25.7	27	33.6	86.3
Japan	2.2	0.5	0.9	3.6
Netherlands	93.7	74.6	57.8	226.1
Norway	8.5	30	45.1	83.6
Sweden	52.7	64.1	100	216.8
Switzerland	7.9	12	14	33.9
U.K.	0.9	0.5	0.3	1.7
U.S.A.	106.7	0	0	106.7

Source: Orozco 1995. Figures in millions of dollars.

In addition to donor countries, international NGOs came to Nicaragua to work on various development projects, such as agricultural cooperative programs and social services for the poor. By the end of 1989, nearly eighty international NGOs were working in Nicaragua on various economic development projects. These groups contributed nearly $100 million over the decade (INICAE 1991, 123).

As the war intensified, international actors actively took positions in the internal conflict which involved a dispute over the meaning of democracy and democratization in Nicaragua. On the one hand, some international actors such as Eastern European countries, NGOs, solidarity organizations, and some Scandinavian countries advocated a notion of democracy as an exercise of sovereignty and self-determination that resided exclusively in the citizenry. In this context, United States policies were criticized as interventionist and obstructionist of those rights. On the other hand, other actors were concerned with the content and process of democracy. For many, this meant accepting the United States and its increasingly dominant and internationally accepted view of democracy summarized in three broad points: universal suffrage, freedom of the market (or capitalism), and anti-communism. In this way, the conflict over the notion of democracy and democratization in Nicaragua took various forms as international actors expressed and mobilized their positions regarding these issues.

Given this scenario, actors sought to promote democracy in different ways. Some, like the members of the so-called Contadora group (Mexico, Panama, Colombia, and Venezuela) participated as mediators in the conflict;

others (Scandinavian and Nordic countries) actively promoted democracy by other means such as foreign aid; and still others pressured Nicaragua to conform to U.S. standards (Nicaraguans in exile and El Salvador). State actors that participated in the conflict included Mexico, Costa Rica, South American democracies, Western European democracies, (Nordic countries on the side of sovereignty, and the leading members of the EEC on the U.S. side), Third World countries from the non-aligned movement, socialist countries including Cuba, the USSR, and socialist bloc countries, and the United States. Other actors included certain foreign national political parties, churches of various denominations (the World Council of Churches, Evangelical organizations, Methodists, etc.), international movements like Amnesty International, and international organizations such as the United Nations, OAS and the European Economic Community (Grabendorf 1992).

In countries experiencing civil wars, international mobilization becomes more challenging given the interconnectedness between peace (security) and democracy (stability). The link between these two goals makes promotion of democracy a more complex process. International actors therefore seek to pressure and support consensus among opposing parties in the areas of security, reconciliation, human rights, and elections (Kumar 1997; Kumar 1998).

The mediation role offered by Costa Rica intertwined peace and democracy. This linkage prevailed and facilitated the transition to democratic installation. The Costa Rican president, Oscar Arias, sought to reconcile Nicaraguan sovereignty and U.S. political interests by offering a peace plan that simultaneously addressed basic security and democracy. International pressure intensified during this stage of the political process and facilitated an eventual opportunity for these actors to support democratic installation and consolidation in the near future.

Internationalization of Democracy in the 1990s

International actors assumed greater roles in influencing politics in Nicaragua, after the end of the Cold War and the 1990 election. International influence and involvement are important categories of analysis in this book. Influence is defined as the effect one actor has on another. Such effect can be measured by looking at the ways in which political practices, institutions, laws, and policies are changed or adjusted to conform to the model of democracy advocated by international actors. International influence thus occurs in relation to the goals (objectives) and means (mechanisms and instruments) employed. In the first case, influence can be exerted to achieve one of two objectives: a) to ensure the success of particular ongoing issue, or b) to shape the nature and/or outcome of an event. These objectives are related to the mechanisms employed by international actors (control, consent, conditionality, challenge, or contagion) and its instruments.

Involvement is defined as any direct or indirect participation by international actors in issues related to another country. Involvement may be direct or indirect, weak, or strong. Direct involvement can range from participation in political and economic events to the administration of projects in the recipient country. Indirect involvement pertains to participation in forums or in multilateral events where the actor's role is secondary. An actor whose involvement is continued and sustained in most national events and has a wide range of political as well as economic projects in a country is a strongly involved actor. An intermediate form of involvement occurs when actors carry out projects predominantly on an economic basis, but choose to limit their involvement in national political events to that of observers. Involvement is weak when actors participate only indirectly in issues related to a given country.

The 1990s are distinctively different from previous decades. International actors now invest resources directly in democracy-oriented projects in Nicaragua and the rest of the world. Bilateral and multilateral donors, international NGOs and other international organizations like the Organization of American States, the EEC and the United Nations all formulate programs to encourage democratization or provide political and diplomatic support for political events and processes crucial to democratization.

David Held's (1995) notion of the globalization of democracy as a process of interconnectedness of values and interests in scope and intensity becomes clear with the Nicaraguan experience. In scope, the range of international actors as well as the issues they address expands constantly. At the same time, these growing numbers of international groups deepen their work building democracy. International NGOs, international organizations and state actors no longer only offer support for democratization through official development assistance, but also implement programs specifically oriented towards democratization. Actors directly and indirectly promote the deepening of democracy by facilitating the empowerment of civil society and individual rights, supporting democratic institutions and local political structures such as municipal governments, monitoring and providing training for electoral suffrage, and directly participating in the internal events of the influenced country.

Actors Promoting Democracy in Nicaragua

In 1997, the International Institute for Democratic and Electoral Assistance

(IDEA 1997), a major international non-profit organization working to assist democracies around the world, carried out a study on democratic assistance programs among major donor countries and organizations (Russell interview 1997). The study showed that bilateral and multilateral donors in Nicaragua had invested resources in a wide range of programs directly related to democracy. Between 1993 and 1997, international donors assisted Nicaragua in a range of projects and invested nearly $170 million to that end.

This support for democracy was varied and not limited to a few actors. Table 4.3 shows that as a percentage of total democracy assistance the U.S. continued to be the major donor in democracy assistance programs, thus reflecting a strong influence on democratic politics in Nicaragua.

Table 4.3 Democracy Assistance Programs by International Donors

Country	Percent
United States	27.00%
European Union	15.00%
Sweden	13.00%
Other	9.00%
Denmark	7.00%
UNDP	6.00%
Norway	5.00%
IDB	4.00%
Germany	3.00%
UNICEF	3.00%
Switzerland	2.00%
Finland	2.00%
Netherlands	2.00%
Canada	2.00%

Source: IDEA, 1997.

However, other bilateral and multilateral donors have also assisted the country in meaningful terms. In fact, combined assistance from Scandinavian countries contributed as much as the U.S. did, and Swedish democracy assistance was the second largest among donor countries. This diversity of assistance contradicts the notion that U.S. aid has remained the single most dominant influencing external force in the country (Robinson 1996). This allocation of resources suggests that democratization has become an important political terrain for international actors to influence other states and societies with their values and interests.

The current perspectives on international involvement in democracy involve a debate between two schools, the 'transitologists' and the critics of transnational capital. According to Stahaler-Sholk (1998) 'transitologists' are a school with an

> emphasis on a moderate middle as agents of reform, and on the international community as positive and significant force for democratization [which] bears many of the hallmarks of the modernization theory and nation-building of yesterday. It assumes a world view in which the United States is a major global promoter of democracy, the Soviet Union was a principal obstacle and the expansion of market-oriented development is a key facilitating condition (1998, 1).

Critics of transnational capital, like Robinson, see democracy promotion as led mainly by the U.S. They do not see an encouragement for an authentic democracy but rather a "new ideology for protecting the interests of transnational elites in an era of globalized production" (Stahaler-Sholk 1998, 1). Transnational capital critics also argue that 'transitologists' tend to privilege order over equality and emphasize electoral procedures, or what has been termed as 'electoral democracy', rather than democracy as a principle of human equality and freedom.

Nicaragua was historically deeply damaged and negatively affected by U.S. influence, especially during the civil war. Nevertheless, the experiences of contemporary Nicargua largely contradict the 'transnational capital' critique of democracy promotion. As the previous table showed, the share of U.S. assistance for democracy competed with that of Western European countries. Moreover, a look at the distribution of foreign assistance shows that electoral aid was only one component of a more diverse perspective and aid package. The details of financial support suggest that electoralism that is, sole reliance on electoral procedures to determine a country's level of democracy, plays only a partial role in notions of democracy among both bilateral and multilateral donors.

Table 4.4 shows the distribution of democracy assistance programs in five sectors: democratization, human rights, local development, elections, and institution building. Democratization programs targeted areas such as empowerment of civil society through civic education, community organizations, and reconciliation strategies among various groups. Human rights programs were oriented towards monitoring rights, training leaders, and educating and advocating civil and political rights to the public at large. Monitoring of rights violations was a key element in securing the democratic transition. Assistance to protect and promote human rights was higher than any other program. Institution building refers to assistance to modernize the legislative and judiciary branches of government, including to train those who work within them. Finally, local development programs seek to strengthen the work of local governments. As the table below shows, total assistance on elections occupied only one-quarter of all programs.

Table 4.4 Assistance for Democracy by Sector

Sector	Percent
Democratization	19.9%
Human Rights	26.6%
Local development	17.0%
Elections	24.7%
Institutions	11.8%

Source: IDEA, 1997.

Even when aid is broken down by regional distribution, electoral assistance is not a main area for the United States or Scandinavian countries, the two major donors. In fact, it is the Western European group that allocates a high percentage of its assistance to elections. This assistance mainly provided technical and training assistance for the elections in the autonomous coastal area and for the national 1996 election.

Table 4.5 Democratic Assistance by Sector and Region or Country

Regions (Except for the U.S. and Canada)	Sector				
	Local development	Institutions	Democratization	Elections	Human Rights
Asia	.	.	.	100.0%	.
Canada	.	.	.	100.0%	.
Joint projects [a]	89.8%	.	3.5%	4.9%	1.8%
Benelux	3.5%	6.2%	7.5%	70.3%	12.5%
Western Europe	25.3%	1.4%	.	54.6%	18.6%
USA	15.2%	14.7%	10.0%	22.9%	37.2%
Multilateral Organizations	4.7%	19.8%	32.8%	8.7%	34.0%
Scandinavian	20.3%	6.9%	27.1%	27.4%	18.2%

Source: IDEA, 1997. [a] Projects carried between the UNDP and a European country.

The IDEA study provided an important overview of much of the international involvement for democracy in Nicaragua. However, one key international multilateral actor not included in the project was the Organization of American States. This institution has participated in Nicaraguan democratic transition in a variety of ways. In particular, the organization worked in two specific areas, one through assistance to demobilized groups and the other through demining the country. These activities were under the direction of the OAS' Unit for the Promotion of Democracy. As the following chapters will show, the OAS played a strong role in encouraging democratic change. Moreover, international NGOs also played a major role in democratization.

Two types of international NGOs are involved in Nicaragua. First, there are those groups who have established a formal residence in Nicaragua and have officially signed cooperation agreements with Nicaragua's external cooperation ministry. Examples of these groups are the Friedrich Ebert Foundation, the Konrad Adenauer Foundation, and the Nicaraguan American Foundation. Second are those groups or organizations that have maintained a relationship with Nicaragua from their main offices in other countries. Examples of the latter are the National Democratic Institute, the Carter Center, and IFES, among others.

Nearly half of those organizations with a formal presence in Nicaragua were active in the country before 1990. Of 162 international NGOs in 1996, 78 of them had been created before 1990. Most of these organizations continue to carry out development-related activities. However, some of their work has an explicit reference to democracy as a condition for social change. Their financial contributions to Nicaragua have been significant, totaling $383 million dollars between 1990 and 1996. Table 4.6 shows the total contribution of NGOs in Nicaragua in this period and the number of organizations operating in the country by 1996.

U.S. based NGOs represent one fifth of all international NGOs in Nicaragua. Groups from Spain and Germany are also actively involved in the country. Many of these organizations work closely with their home-country international aid agencies as administrators of various programs. However, they also use independent funds to fulfill their goals.

International NGOs involved with or in Nicaragua but that do not have an established residence in the country are harder to track. Some, however, are well-known organizations. For example, American organizations like the National Democratic Institute, the International Republican Institute and the Carter Center have an international orientation and have paid a lot of attention to Nicaragua. The NDI, for example, participated in forging an agenda about civil-military relations which later gave way to a debate about a military code in the country. The Carter Center has been a major actor in the country. It has mediated disputes over the property issue and supported the electoral process of 1990 and 1996. As a post-conflict democracy, Nicaragua has been a major focus of interest among international organizations concerned with democratization and stability in the developing world. As will be observed in the following chapter, these organizations played major roles in Nicaragua's transition.

Table 4.6 International NGOs in Nicaragua: Distribution by Financial Contributions and Number of Organizations (1990-1996)

Country of origin	Value of cooperation (in millions of dollars)	Number of organizations	Percent from total	Value per organization
United States	79.5	32	19.88%	2.48
Belgium	40.7	7	4.35%	5.81
Germany	35.9	11	6.83%	3.26
Sweden	30.8	7	4.35%	4.4
Canada	28.5	10	6.21%	2.85
Norway	27.2	7	4.35%	3.89
Denmark	26.1	5	3.11%	5.22
Netherlands	24.9	5	3.11%	4.98
Italy	20.7	6	3.73%	3.45
Austria	15.6	19	11.80%	0.82
Spain	15.4	17	10.56%	0.91
Switzerland	15.2	11	6.83%	1.38
United Kingdom	10.5	14	8.70%	0.75
Finland	8.9	6	3.73%	1.48
France	3.2	4	2.48%	0.8
Total	383.1	161	100.00%	2.38

Source: Nicaraguan External Cooperation Ministry 1996.

The political process in Nicaragua in the 1990s was significantly influenced by international actors. They pressured, supported, or used other means to democratize the country by offering mechanisms to maintain peace after the war, stability, respect for civil and political rights, and political empowerment in a deeply ideologically divided and undemocratic society.

Since 1989, international mobilization put energies into reaching negotiated outcomes that allowed for demobilizing warring forces, reducing the military budget, negotiating political reforms, and developing local government and civil society. As the next chapter will show, Nicaragua experienced five major political developments, many of which were directly related to its progress towards further democratization. Peace negotiations, power repositioning among leading elites, pluralization of society, demilitarization, and state reform were major developments experienced in the first seven years of democratic rule. International action influenced the move towards democratic rule in many of these events

International and Domestic Linkages

One of the main arguments of the 'transnational capital' critique is that promotion of democracy has a top-down and vertical nature, so that local elites and organizations function as agents of capitalism. Another critique is that democracy promotion is dictated by polyarchic assumptions about democracy. A closer look at international interactions over democracy reveals a more complex picture. Although power is a dominant factor in explaining U.S. interests, the reception of aid and assistance from the U.S. and elsewhere occurs in a web of bargaining and interdependence. One can thus argue that, while the U.S. seeks to set the tone of democratization, it has to bargain with various actors, both foreign and domestic. Moreover, while U.S. foreign policy interests are not always consistent with democratic values, thus often betraying values the U.S. advocates in pro-democracy programs, the interests and identities of U.S. functionaries are not monolithic or always self-interested. In other words, pointing to the U.S. as an international actor may be misleading, as there may be contesting interests among State Department personnel, AID officers, the Congress and embassies within this political unit called the U.S.

Because democratic issues now concern both domestic and foreign terrains, they assume an intermestic character. Actors need to establish linkages and seek 'partners' to achieve their goals. One sees a complex interplay of cooperation and bargaining over democratic issues among the various domestic and foreign actors. Donors, bilateral and multilateral, maintain strong links with local governments and broad sectors of civil society, while international civil society simultaneously maintains connections with donors and domestic actors. This development will be evident in the analysis of the 1996 elections and the study of the development of civil society in following chapters.

Although the establishment of partnerships does not preclude the distorted imposition of power, the distribution of power is not fixed or static, but rather is in a constant state of flux depending on the actors' needs, interests, and identities. Therefore, hierarchical influence is only one possibility among other outcomes.

International action is also not only of one ideological kind. The large array of actors view democracy in different ways. Their understandings of rule by the people vary from the importance of providing and guaranteeing specific civil and political rights, to the promotion of development. Thus, the flow of assistance or involvement in internal events is not unidirectional in the orientation of one actor's wishes, but rather will depend on the interplay between needs, views, and bargaining among partners and other actors' positions.

Thus, democracy becomes another political space in which international actors look to exert influence. The growth of international activity is reflected in the case of democracy. International civil society organizations, such as foundations or centers for the study and promotion of democracy, party internationals, diasporic movements, and other groups, have made democracy a subject of concern for the activities of their organizations and mobilized their resources to make their values influential. In this sense, the international dimension of democracy is the expression of interests and identities of a growing number of international actors in the area of democracy. This expression is manifested through their influence over issues and events under different conditions and circumstances. Because there is no necessary convergence of interests around democracy, actors involved in promoting democracy reflect contesting views as they invest tangible resources in the democratization process.

Chapter 5

Negotiating Peace and Holding Elections

The civil war in Nicaragua was an international as well as an internal conflict. The hostilities were variously understood as part of the East-West Cold War confrontation (Wiarda 1987; Leiken 1984) or as another confrontation between the northern colossus and its victims to the south (Norsworthy and Robinson 1987; Kornbluh 1987). In either case, international players had made clear that peace and democracy must come to Nicaragua. The international community expressed these concerns in various multilateral and bilateral forums. At the United Nations, for example, resolutions were passed to help alleviate the regional conflict, bring peace, and democratize Nicaragua.

International pressures to end the war and introduce democracy to Nicaragua showed a concerted effort previously observed during the struggle to overthrow Somoza. International pressures took different forms, but were particularly influenced by the U.S. goal to remove the Sandinistas from power by military means. The United States presented this objective as a prerequisite for peace and democracy. Thus, a dominant feature of the conflict was the U.S. use of political and military control as its mechanisms of influence.

As the first section of this chapter will show, the U.S. position did not prevail. Actors such as the Costa Rican government of Oscar Arias, the OAS, Western European countries and the U.N. applied pressure to end the war through negotiated means. Their support for ending the war in Nicaragua via a simultaneous regional peace agreement proved an incentive to the Sandinista National Liberation Front (FSLN) to negotiate peace. This option prevailed over both the U.S. and exiled Nicaraguans' pro-military position. International mobilization stepped up as the violence and instability in Nicaragua increased.

The second section of this chapter identifies international efforts to pressure the Sandinistas to hasten the elections after peace was negotiated and to allow international monitoring to supervise fair and free elections conforming to international standards. While the United States sought to shape the nature and the outcome of the electoral process, the broader international community sought to ensure the success of a free and fair election. Although peace negotiations and elections were two separate events, the international community linked them as a measure to achieve stability in the region.

Pressures to Negotiate Peace in Nicaragua

Two years after the triumph of the revolution, civil war arose from a series of political, economic, social, and ethnic conflicts. In 1979, the Sandinista government created a solid political-military structure prepared to defend the country against aggression. The war against the Sandinistas initially emerged as a counterrevolutionary project organized by former members of Somoza's National Guard who wanted to recuperate their lost power. As internal and external tensions increased, however, the conflict turned into a broader civil war with international dimensions. The internationalization of the conflict and its transformation from a counterrevolutionary project into a civil war complicated the crisis and delayed a negotiated settlement.

Arguing that the Sandinista revolution involved a Soviet conspiracy, the Reagan administration initiated a well-organized mission to create and support an anti-Sandinista movement. Although sporadic armed confrontation had started as early as 1980, by late 1983 full-scale warfare had developed, in large part due to a U.S.-sponsored war against the Sandinista government.

Because the revolution was not a fully democratic project, it hurt many people in ways that encouraged them to fight, especially as other opportunities for dissent or protest were narrowed or closed. The peasantry in particular was unhappy about the Sandinista agrarian reform and their overt anti-clericalism. The state had enormous reach into and influences over people's lives and was partisan in its approach. As Rouquie (1994, 219, author's translation) notes:

It is true that Nicaragua was never a tropical GDR [German Democratic Republic], nor a copy of Cuba. . . but the FSLN undoubtedly created the institutions of a totalitarian state. . . . The police and the army were officially Sandinista, that is, partisan and in some way similar to Somoza's National Guard, and there is no doubt that the state was intermeshed with the party.

The heightened tensions between Sandinistas and the opposition produced the full-scale civil war that by 1986 left considerable losses and destruction all over the country. Thousands of civilians and combatants died in the fighting. Hundreds of thousands of people left their homes and migrated both internally and abroad. The economy and infrastructure were seriously affected. The table below summarizes an inventory of some of these losses.

The war, together with other conditions, it began to have a negative impact on the Nicaraguan capacity to resist, thus raising the costs of continued fighting. It became clear to all sides that the war had to stop. Efforts were made to redirect the armed conflict toward peace via dialogue and negotiation.

Table 5.1 Human and Economic Costs of the War

Human Costs [a]	
Internally Displaced	over 250,000
Refugees	over 200,000
Dead	29,270
Wounded	18,012
Kidnaped/Captured	10,449
Total Victims	57,731
Economic costs [b]	$9,087,700,000

Source: Norsworthy 1990, 59; Dunkerley 1994, 47.
[a] Includes military and civilian casualties. [b] Economic costs include material damages, lost production from the war, and the cost of the trade and credit embargo.

During the civil war, the government refused to negotiate with the contras, whom it condemned as "paid mercenaries of the Reagan administration" (Cortés Domínguez 1990, 47). The contras, on the other hand, saw a military solution as the only way to remove the Sandinistas. After the August 1987 regional peace agreements, however, the Sandinistas offered to negotiate with the contras (Goodfellow and Morrell 1992, 275). After years of civil war, what were the forces leading to this decision? Why did the Nicaraguan rebels accept the Sandinistas' offer to negotiate? What role did the internal opposition, the United States, Central American countries, and other international actors play in helping to achieve an end to the war? These questions need to be answered in explaining the negotiating process.

The Search for a Negotiated Solution to the Internal Conflict.

Throughout the 1980s, Nicaragua was offered opportunities to find a negotiated solution to the civil war. The Latin American countries' offer to mediate, channeled through the Contadora group's peace initiative, was one major attempt at regional conflict resolution (Wehr and Lederach 1991, 89). This and other proposals were undermined by the degree of polarization among the parties, and the unwillingness of national actors to negotiate.

Until 1987, when Oscar Arias of Costa Rica introduced a negotiating formula to achieve peace in the region, Nicaragua lacked a path to conflict resolution. To a greater or lesser extent, the Arias peace plan offered each party in the conflict incentives and guarantees to end the war and regional conflict. Due to Costa Rica's proximity to Nicaragua and its close relationship with the United States, it had become a party to the conflict and had vested interests in the region's future (Sojo 1991; Rojas Aravena 1990). Thus, Costa Rica enjoyed a particular position that allowed it simultaneously to be both a mediator and a party in negotiations.

The Arias proposal linked peace, democracy, and development into a plan that was less costly than continued fighting (Rojas Aravena 1988, 118). That the proposal originated from Central America gave it significant added legitimacy. Further validity derived from the many benefits the plan offered for an array of domestic and international actors. Although the Arias initiative and the negotiation process had a regional application, its main objective was to first make Nicaragua negotiate peace.

There were various actors involved in the negotiation, either as parties or as mediators or facilitators. These actors included the Sandinistas, the contras, and Nicaragua's Central American neighbors, as key negotiators, and the United States, Western European and Latin American countries as allied or mediators. The various actors are examined in turn.

The Sandinista government The Arias plan's incentives offered were necessary, but not sufficient, to establish a peace process. Material as well as "ideal" objectives were vital in creating the incentives to negotiate. William Zartman (1991, 16) has argued that one important factor that informs the decision to negotiate is the existence of a hurting stalemate, a condition of deadlock in which neither party can win the war. In the case of the Nicaraguan civil war, by 1987 the Sandinista government had defeated the contra objective of overthrowing the Nicaraguan government. Yet, a strategic defeat, as the Sandinistas called it, was not enough to stop the climate of political instability in rural areas. At least four factors explain Nicaragua's decision to take advantage of the Arias initiative: the elevated costs of the war, the economic crisis resulting from government mismanagement, international pressure to democratize (including from sources other than the United States and Central America), and demands for democratization from the internal opposition.

The war against the Sandinista government not only constrained the Sandinistas' policy choices but also, over time, created a fatigue that limited the government's ability to continue fighting the contras while implementing its new social policies. The regime's continued resolve to further the revolution without seriously listening to internal social demands for change eventually eroded its popular base. Support for the Sandinistas began to decline as citizens started to question the symbolism behind the revolutionary rhetoric and people demanded an end to the war. This decline in support undermined Sandinista claims that defense of the revolution justified the war and negotiating with the contras dishonored the memory of those fallen at the rebel's hands.

Economic crisis and mismanagement were another problem. The war had affected the whole economy, not only the rural towns that were the center of contra activity. Continued sabotage of electrical plants and development projects raised the costs of economic growth. Between 1981 and 1985, for example, the contras undertook 640 attacks on economic targets, causing millions of dollars in losses (Vergara Meneses 1987, 170). The presence of contra units near populated rural areas with important commercial centers led to massive internal migrations that depopulated those areas. More than 500,000 Nicaraguans were internally and externally displaced during, or as a result of, the war. The death toll rose to more than 45,000 and there were hundreds of thousands of wounded (Lake 1990, 106-113). These costs added to the immense price of the U.S. embargo. After two years of the embargo trade with the United States and the rest of the world decreased by 62 percent. The decline especially affected imports of American capital goods. In addition, state enterprises, land distribution, social subsidies, and credit suffered from serious administration and management problems that directly affected fiscal and monetary health and stability. Inflation skyrocketed to four digits, reaching 1,347.4% in 1987. Hyperinflation was the result of government financing of the war (military spending accounted for 50 % of its budget), and of mismanagement. Money supply far exceeded material reserves and national production capacity, and the maintenance of three different exchange rates created an artificial economy. As a result, wages were far lower than prices. Discontent over the handling of the economy was especially evident among state workers, who represented one-third of the labor force, and the urban population, which was most affected by the crisis. By 1987, this growing discontent was manifested openly and would eventually influence the voters' decision in the 1990 elections (Conroy 1990).

To these forces, it is important to add the international pressures to become democratic. The Sandinistas received substantial support from Western European countries and some Latin American countries who saw in the revolution an experiment in participatory democracy. During the 1980s, European aid to Nicaragua came to represented 50% of the region's total foreign aid to Central America (Orozco 1995). The donors did, however, link development to democracy, and stressed that a country without respect for basic civil and political rights could not go far as a free polity. Peace initiatives from Spain, Nordic countries, and members of the EEC made it clear that aid should be tied to democratic development to some extent (Durán 1988).

Finally, the internal and legal political opposition, made up of the opposition political parties and private enterprise, re-articulated its demands for political opening. The opposition organized a coalition of political parties, private businesses, and trade unions which insisted upon democratic changes and questioned the legitimacy and popularity of Sandinismo. Along with this opposition, other signs of dissent manifested disenchantment with the war and the economy. These conditions combined to increase the attractiveness of alternative regional solutions to end the political and economic crisis, as well as American pressures against the Sandinista government.

Central America A common incentive for Costa Rica, El Salvador, Honduras, and Guatemala to negotiate the regional peace plan was the belief that a solution to the regional crisis depended on national reconciliation and democratization in Nicaragua. As largely undemocratic states (with the exception of Costa Rica), their basic compromise was to accept internal democratization themselves while pressuring Nicaragua. (This accommodation came despite the fact that these countries already claimed to be democratic, and had the support of the United States as "proof" of this status.) These countries reached a consensus that, although the peace plan committed all five nations to comply, the primary focus was on Nicaragua (Norsworthy 1990, 42). To Costa Rica, the peace plan was an opportunity to restore its international credibility, damaged after accusations that it had allowed itself to be used by contras to wage war against Nicaragua. Costra Rica's use of its moral authority as the only real democracy in the region in turn gave the country more prestige (Moreno 1994, 83-86).

The Contras Just as the Sandinista government was persuaded to negotiate by a number of factors, the contra rebels also faced various issues that influenced their support for negotiation. The contras originated from the ranks of the former National Guard exiled in Miami and Tegucigalpa, Honduras. Since 1980, they were engaged in a battle against the Nicaraguan government. Initially they received CIA assistance to form an 'arms interdiction contingent' (supposedly to block Sandinista arms shipments to El Salvador's FMLN guerrillas). Later, the Reagan administration backed and supported them as freedom fighters against a "communist Nicaragua." In 1981 the contras formed the Nicaraguan Democratic Forces (FDN) comprising three organizations, the National Liberation Army, the Revolutionary Nicaraguan Alliance, and the September 15 Legion (Rouquie 1994, 205). All were made up of former National Guard members. That same year the FDN joined actions with other organizations - Miskitos, Sumus, and Ramas (MISURA) and Miskitos, Sumus, Ramas, Sandinista All Together (MISURASTA), operating from Honduras, and Revolutionary Democratic Alliance (ARDE), based in Costa Rica. MISURA and MISURASATA were made up of disaffected indigenous groups of the Atlantic Coast of Nicaragua whom the Sandinistas had attempted to integrate by force. ARDE was a counterrevolutionary force led by a former member of the FSLN that invited civilians to oppose the way Nicaragua was being governed. By 1985 the counterrevolution was reorganized integrating a few other groups, amounting to a total of 15,500 members. In part because their leadership was associated with human rights abuses and with Somoza's former National Guard, the contras changed their name to the Nicaraguan Democratic Resistance (NR) in 1985. The Nicaraguan Resistance was first led by civilian leaders like Alfredo César, who had previously worked for the Sandinista government and belonged to the middle class, but later influenced also by former National Guard members (Vergara Meneses 1987,175-177).

A number of factors worked to change the contras' stance on negotiations. First, they had suffered a military defeat. Although the NR could (and did) enter Nicaragua from Honduras and attack important towns in rural areas, by 1987 its military power was not sufficient either to defeat Sandinismo or to demand fundamental changes (Moreno 1990, 127-128). Second, as discontent with Sandinismo grew, different groups, including peasants and members of the middle class, joined the contra forces, bringing alternative strategies to confront Sandinismo. The dominant contra faction, led by former National Guard member Enrique Bermúdez, was challenged by peasant and middle-class factions that began to view negotiation as an alternative way to deal with the Nicaraguan government (Opazo and Fernández 1990, 218). Third, despite Reagan's support for the contras, events in the United States reduced the likelihood of long-term U.S. support for the contras. The Iran-Contra scandal revealed the existence of illegal transfers of military equipment to the contras purchased with U.S. funds and directed by U.S. officials in the CIA and National Security Council. This incident, plus the growing opposition to the contras in U.S. public opinion polls and from grassroots organizations, was reflected in the congressional refusal to approve an aid package in February 1988. Members of Congress cited the contras' limited operational gains and their reputation for human rights abuses (Arnson 1989, 205-206). The Honduran government also expressed dissatisfaction with the contra presence in its territory and began pressuring the U.S. and the rebels to end the situation (Schulz and Schulz 1994, 227-233). These three factors prompted the contras to negotiate peace (or, as it turned out, their partial defeat.)

The United States One of the major obstacles to finding a negotiated solution to the conflict in Nicaragua was that the United States had rejected negotiating with Nicaragua. Any kind of accord, regional or bilateral, ran the risk of being boycotted or negatively affected by American disapproval. The U.S. eventual decision to support a negotiated settlement under the Arias proposal was a strategic move targeting Nicaragua. Although the regional peace plan proposed by Arias was not the Reagan administration's preferred choice (the United States had presented a bipartisan peace plan focusing only on Nicaragua but was rejected by the Central American presidents), the United States could shape it to focus only on Nicaraguan compliance. The agreement thus became a bargaining tool to gain more concessions from the Sandinistas (Sojo 1991, 54).

Western Europe Western European and Latin American countries were key actors in promoting regional negotiation. These parties also saw Nicaragua as the keystone to peace in the area. Western Europe's move to encourage negotiations was explained by European domestic and international concerns. Civil society organizations in Europe, especially those which opposed intervention and supported human rights and democracy, as well as the party internationals, encouraged an end to the war. More broadly, most European countries valued safeguarding of the "sovereignty and independence of any country" (Duran 1988, 35).

Western European countries also sought to support peace and democracy in the region as alternatives to Washington's one-sided position. Claude Cheysson, Commissioner for the European Community (EC) and its relations with Central America, expressed the importance of the Community's efforts to "halt violence and instability and promote justice, economic development and respect for both human rights and democratic liberties in this part of the world" (Smith 1995, 95). Although members of the European community did not confront the United States directly on its Central America policy, they appealed to "all countries with links to and interests in the region" to play a constructive role. In 1987, Cheysson warned the EC members of the possible "slide into totalitarianism" by countries in Central America and argued that military pressure was not the way to prevent this trend (Smith 1995, 96). These statements were designed to express the European Community's position on democratizing Nicaragua and oppose the U.S. embargo and aid to the contras.

Although European countries were ideologically divided over support for Nicaragua, they all agreed with the European Commission's appeal for negotiation. Together, the European member states promoted a consensus among Nicaraguan leaders to pursue peace negotiations. Their efforts were explicit in the Commission's political support for the viability of the Arias peace plan and in their development assistance to help Nicaragua recover from the war.

Latin America Latin American efforts were divided among three groups: diplomatic initiatives by the Contadora group, individual countries' foreign policies, and OAS initiatives. The Contadora group was formed in 1983 by the foreign ministers of Colombia, Mexico, Panama, and Venezuela at a meeting on the Panamanian island of Contadora. The group sought to prevent the continuation of warfare as well as to assert independence from the United States (Méndez Asencio 1987). Its diplomatic efforts concentrated on reducing regional security threats and military escalation; however, due to divergent perceptions over where these threats resided, little agreement was possible about how to proceed in solving the Central America conflict. To El Salvador, Honduras and to a lesser extent, Costa Rica, Nicaragua's regime was a threat to the region because of its non-democratic character, its adoption of 'foreign' ideologies and insurgence, and its relationship with the Soviet bloc. To Nicaragua, the threat to the region was U.S. intervention supported by Central American countries. This difference in the perception of threat was critical in defining the failure of Contadora's peace efforts. By 1985, the Contadora group was joined by a support group made up of Brazil, Argentina, Peru, and Uruguay. These countries continued to support Contadora's efforts and a Latin American solution to the conflict (Méndez Asencio 1987, 171).

In January 1987, members of the OAS, the UN, Contadora and its support group visited the five Central American countries to encourage the signing of Contadora latest version of a peace agreement. However, the agreement had already been rejected by Costa Rica, Honduras, and El Salvador--also called the iron triangle group known for their solid opposition to Nicaragua and inflexible positions toward negotiation before the Arias plan was passed. Frustration with the lack of commitment was expressed by Javier Perez de Cuellar, then UN Secretary General, who emphasized that a negotiated solution to the regional conflict could only occur if the parties agreed to compromise. Despite the failure of Contadora's peace efforts, Latin American countries continued to support peace initiatives. The Contadora group had transformed itself into an eight-member group within the OAS to support the Arias plan. The OAS also was active in encouraging a peaceful solution to the crisis in Nicaragua. Although the institution had suffered a setback during the Argentine-United Kingdom conflict over the Malvinas Islands, the OAS continued its efforts to maintain an inter-American consensus over issues such as ending the Central American wars and introducing democracy. Latin Americans saw Nicaragua as the steppingstone to solving the crisis. The OAS was entrusted with the mandate of providing "every assistance to the Central American Governments in their efforts to achieve peace" (Caminos and Lavalle 1989, 397). In that context, the organization offered its mediating offices as well as support for the Contadora peace efforts. On various occasions the OAS and UN joined to express their joint concern for the deterioration of the crisis and "outlined the services that their respective organizations, singly or jointly, could render with a view to promoting the efforts of the two groups" (Caminos and Lavalle 1989, 398). The Arias peace agreement requested the Secretaries-General of the UN and OAS to participate as members of the International Verification and Follow-up Commission (CIAV), which would oversee the agreements. Sergio Caramagna, head of CIAV from 1990 to 1997 (when he was appointed OAS Ambassador to Nicaragua), pointed out that "the pacification efforts were not authored by the OAS, instead the OAS added itself to a peace process that was based on the political will of the parties and in a search to end the conflict" (Caramagna interview 1997).

The Negotiated Settlements in Nicaragua

Nicaragua's experience with negotiation had grown through the four years of meetings and dealings with Central American countries to negotiate agreements proposed by the Contadora group. Its main achievements, however, occurred after the failed efforts of Contadora. Nicaragua reached at least six major agreements to end the country's civil war, of which Esquipulas II was the first. The agreements aimed at two basic points: ending the civil war by disarming and demobilizing the contras, and democratizing Nicaragua. In this context, the Esquipulas agreements represented the most important breakthrough: they bound Nicaragua to comply with specific points, while each point in the agreement was a conduit to negotiate further aspects of the civil war.

With Esquipulas II, Oscar Arias changed the Contadora focus on security and close monitoring to a linkage between regional democracy and peace in a more simplified negotiation framework. Arias presented the formula in San José, Costa Rica in February 1987 to the presidents of El Salvador, Honduras, and Guatemala. Arias argued that democracy was the main issue: "The essence of the peace plan was democracy as a requisite for peace. There were people who, because of repeated violations of their right to vote, had taken up arms in Central America" (interview, 1997). If a consensus was reached on the peace plan between the regional allies, it would then be presented to the international community to win support introduced as a basis of negotiations in Nicaragua (Moreno 1994, 87). Although the tactical objective of the peace plan was primarily to bring democracy to Nicaragua, its diplomatic and political objective was to de-escalate the internal wars in the region. The plan was binding on each Central American country, including Costa Rica.

At that meeting in San José, the four presidents supported the peace plan. This first step signified a fundamental change in the regional peace process. It shifted the peace initiative to the Central American countries from other external actors--including the United States, whose interests were not served by the plan. The initiative represented a major display of regional autonomy toward the United States whose foreign policy had dominated decisions in the region (Bendaña 1992, 3). That feature of the plan, and its regional character, became the two most powerful attractions for the Sandinistas to accept it. In addition, the plan provided important self-enforcing mechanisms that built confidence among the parties, Nicaragua in particular.

The agreement was later signed in August 1987 in Esquipulas, Guatemala. It was composed of eleven points and contained six basic objectives: a cease-fire, national reconciliation (dialogue and amnesty), democratization (through free elections, freedom of expression, and a process of pluralism with respect to social justice and human rights), an end to aid to insurgent movements (whether through providing them material resources or allowing them in to the territory to attack a neighbor's state), refugee assistance, and development support. These objectives did not differ radically from the February proposal that Arias had presented to his allies.

Nicaragua was especially pleased by the enforcement formula, which was composed of four elements: calendarization, verification, simultaneity, and symmetry (Gomariz 1988, 67-70; Rojas Aravena 1988, 118). The formula demanded a process of compliance with each point by a certain date and was subject to verification. The timetable stipulated the implementation of the agreement and its evaluation. Ninety days after the agreement was signed, on 7 November 1987, the countries were to comply with amnesty, cease-fire, democratization, termination of aid to irregular and insurrectional forces, and the denial of territory for the purposes of attacking other states. Thirty days after the November deadline a verification commission would review the progress of compliance with the agreements, and thirty days later the Central American presidents would meet to review this commission's report. Verification was delegated to international observers (members of the Contadora group and OAS and UN organs), who would determine the degree of compliance among members. Verification became an important institutional mechanism in three areas: at the local level through the work of national reconciliation commissions; regionally through the Executive Committee, a consulting group among presidents; and internationally through the work of the verification commission of (Child 1992, 47).

The agreement also called for simultaneous compliance. This meant, for example, that Nicaragua as well as the other Central American countries would begin democratization at the same time as they ceased any military action against insurgent or rebel forces. This provision of symmetry among countries was a critical part of the Esquipulas II agreement. As Opazo and Fernández explain, "no country was attributed responsibility in the genesis, development and resolution of the crisis. [The agreement thus opened] the possibility of a new pragmatism that would allow all countries to be treated with the same yardstick" (Opazo and Fernandez 1990, 192).

The principle of symmetry was important to Nicaragua since it meant that the other four Central American countries were recognizing the legitimacy of its government. However, another element of symmetry operated at the internal level. The countries were given the responsibility of compliance in accordance with their internal conditions in their countries. In this context Nicaragua could place more emphasis on refugee settlement and reconciliation than on democratization and free elections by arguing that the country had already engaged in a democratization process including elections in 1984. Symmetry also constituted the main bargaining tool for Central American countries to pressure Nicaragua to comply in full with the peace agreements.

Although the Esquipulas II agreement did not end the conflict, it represented two important advances. For the first time, the countries involved agreed to terminate their conflict by assuming individual responsibility to end the regional conflict. Each country's participation influenced other countries, Nicaragua in particular, to comply with the agreements. Thus, bargaining came to determine the course of future negotiations. Each point also represented a window of opportunity for a continued negotiation process in each of the areas where peace was absent. Thus, the negotiation process did not end with Esquipulas II; rather, it began in August 1987 and culminated with the April and June 1990 Managua agreements over demobilization and security conditions for the Nicaraguan contras. The bargaining power and the window of opportunity for future concessions that Esquipulas II offered were the key to gradual change in the political scenario of negotiations in Nicaragua.

In fact, compliance with the agreements also meant the establishment of dialogue with internal and external opposition groups. The Nicaragua government agreed to a cease fire with the contras, whose power base had been dramatically eroded both politically and militarily. This decision led to the Sapoa cease-fire agreement, in which both parties stopped fighting while talks on the democratization of Nicaragua began (Child 1992, 54). Although the contras violated the cease-fire, the Sandinistas did not reply militarily as they contemplated their compliance to Costa Rican pressures of not breaking the cease-fire agreement against potentially punitive United States pressures for more democratization in Nicaragua in the case of fighting the contras back. In this context, and because the electoral climate in the United States had caused suspense over the future of U.S. policy in the region, 1988 became a year in which Costa Rica continued pressuring Nicaragua to reach a cease-fire with the contras and open more dialogue with the internal opposition. As a result Nicaragua kept the unilateral cease-fire until November 1988.

Three months later, in Costa del Sol, El Salvador, Nicaragua agreed to hold elections in February 1990, thus forwarding the date nine months from November 1990 as originally scheduled. This pledge to hold early elections was followed months later with an agreement with the internal opposition to implement a series of changes in the electoral law to guarantee fair elections (Moreno 1994, 110; Cortes 1990, 91). This decision was accompanied by various other political changes. First, the Nicaraguan government agreed to invite international observers from the OAS and UN to monitor the progress of the electoral process. Second, the electoral law was reformed to allow for the legalization of new political parties and permit external funding of political parties. Third, the media law was changed to adjust to the previous regulations as well as to allow the opposition media access during the campaign. Fourth, former National Guard prisoners held since 1980 would be pardoned and released (Costa del Sol Agreement 1989). Other changes included a moratorium on military service, the elimination of the Public Order and Security Law, and reform of police jurisdictions.

At Tela, Honduras, a week after the agreement with the internal opposition, Nicaragua was able to obtain a major concession. The Central American leaders agreed to speed up the demobilization of contras in Honduran territory and called upon the United Nations to observe and monitor the process of repatriation and disarmament (Cavallini 1989, 11). This later led to the mandate for the creation of the United Nations Mission in Central America (ONUCA) whose role was complemented by the UN's activities in monitoring the elections in Nicaragua (for which purpose UNUVEN was created). The sheer pressure on Nicaragua gradually produced full compliance with the two major U.S. and Central American and U.S. goals in Nicaragua: removing the Sandinistas from office and ending the war. (The fact that the first goal was achieved through the electoral process was an additional advantage for opponents of the Sandinistas.) The table below summarizes the various peace agreements Nicaragua signed between 1987 and 1990.

Table 5.2. Negotiations in Nicaragua: Main Agreements Reached

Date	Nature	Outcome	Parties
August 1987, Esquipulas II, Guatemala	! Regional peace agreement.	! Established a framework for future negotiations and a strategic mechanism to pressure Nicaragua.	Costa Rica, El Salvador, Guatemala, Honduras, Nicaragua.
March 1988, Sapoa Agreement-- Nicaragua	! Cease-fire agreement between contras and government.	! Contras agree to cease-fire while conversations with Nicaraguan government begin. ! Contras violate agreement.	Nicaraguan government and contras. (Church acted as mediator.)
February 1989, Caracas, Venezuela and Tesoro Beach, El Salvador	! Agreement to forward elections ! Contras urged to disarm.	! Latin America puts pressure on Nicaragua to democratize. Nicaragua complies.	Nicaragua, other Latin American countries,.
August 1989, Managua Agreement & Tela Agreement, Honduras	! Sandinistas open dialogue with Nicaraguan opposition. ! Honduras agrees to disband contras from its territory. ! UN receives mandate to observe disarming and disbandment of contras.	! Concession from Honduras in exchange for Nicaragua's withdrawal of a demand before the International Court of Justice regarding Honduras allowing the use of its territory for attacks against Nicaragua. ! Limited scope, but sends strong message to contras. ! International organizations are set to begin monitoring and mobilization of contras: ONUCA is created. ! Dialogue begins after years of sterile discussions.	Honduras and Nicaragua main parties. UN and OAS as monitors.
March 1990, Toncontin, Hon. Agreement	Demobilization and security matters of contras.	! Beginning of demobilization negotiations with contras.	Sandinista government and contras.

| April 1990, Managua, Nic. Agreements | Demobilization and security guarantees of Nicaraguan Resistance. | ! Contras begin to demobilize.
! Contras lose power in negotiation. | NR-Sandinista and Chamorro government. |

Pressure for Free and Fair Elections

The Sandinista decision to move up the election date came as a welcome surprise to the international community. It represented an important sign of political opening in a country that had restricted civic and political liberties and exacerbated national tensions in the name of resistance to 'Yankee imperialism'.

International pressures on Nicaragua focused on guaranteeing a free and fair electoral process and the continuity of democratic institutionalization. Yet tension existed between the interests of the United States and the contras on the one hand, and those of the rest of the international community on the other. The former sought to shape the nature and the outcome of the political process, whereas the latter pursued peaceful and successful elections.

The 1990 Nicaraguan political process was important for the country and the international community. It was no coincidence that the election was taking place during the end of the Cold War and the development of globalization. Nicaragua became both a cause and an effect of an emerging international development: widespread international electoral monitoring. International actors sought to situate themselves on a continuum, with collectively enforcing an emerging practice of widespread elections into a shared norm (free elections and democracy) at one end and seeking themselves to interpret such norms to their best interest at the other end. Although the defeat of Sandinismo--or, more important, the success of an electoral victory that facilitated a democratic transition--was primarily influenced by U.S. interests, the outcome was welcomed by international actors as a sign of the legitimacy of the election process.

International Pressures

The electoral process that Nicaragua opened to international scrutiny marked an important change in world politics: It was the first time that a sovereign nation invited other actors to monitor its political performance. If generalized international pressure for democracy was, in Rosenau's (1997, 264) words, "an erratic norm-building process," this invitation was to "introduce wide cracks in the armor of national sovereignty." Nicaragua was thus the cause and effect of what later would become an international exercise in promoting democracy.

International actors had various perspectives about ways to make democracy possible. Their differences can be reduced to two major points of view: that of the United States, the exiles and contras, on the one hand, and that of Costa Rica and other major international actors such as the OAS, UN, and the European Community, on the other. The United States shaped the nature and the outcome of the electoral process by helping to create an opposition group with a unified voice and a representative and charismatic leader, and by providing significant financial and logistical support. At the same time, the U.S. applied diplomatic pressure for Sandinista compliance with the rules of the political process and protections for the contras. The broader international community tried to influence Nicaraguan politics by ensuring the success of the electoral process. To that end, international monitoring took place before, during, and after the electoral contest.

It is important to highlight that Nicaragua's transition occurred during a period of major international changes including a global process of democratization. For example, the Esquipulas II agreement influenced not only Nicaragua but El Salvador as well. November 1989 marked the Salvadoran guerrillas' final offensive and their determination to seek a negotiated solution to their conflict. Paraguayan dictator Alfredo Stroessner was peacefully overthrown after more than thirty years of dictatorial rule. In South Africa, a process of democratization via liberalization of racial restrictions had begun. Conversations between Mandela and the government developed further with the DeKlerk presidency, leading to Mandela's release in 1990. These events had a direct effect on Nicaraguans, as did the Soviet bloc's policy changes and the subsequent collapse of the USSR. With these changes, the Sandinistas lost their financial aid from the Eastern bloc, one of the regime's major bases of support. Nearer Central America, the new Bush administration adopted more pragmatic postures in U.S. foreign policy. Nonetheless, the invasion of Panama and the removal of General Manuel Antonio Noriega was a sign of continued American military presence and a reminder of a potential U.S. threat.

U.S. Intervention in the Election

U.S. involvement in promoting democracy in Nicaragua marked a break with U.S. policy in the 1980s. The Reagan administration's position on Nicaragua sought complete removal of the Sandinistas from power. While Reagan's discourse berated the Sandinistas' lack of democracy, in practice, the administration's dislike originated from the regime's nationalist stance and the security threat the U.S. intelligence community perceived it represented. In fact, in early bilateral talks and up until the 1984 Manzanillo talks between the U.S. and Nicaragua, the issues under discussion were limited to security concerns, such as the delivery of arms to Salvadoran guerrillas, their training on Nicaraguan soil, and arms build-up by the Sandanista government. Carothers (1991, 100) notes that when U.S. State Department official "Thomas Enders negotiated with the Sandinista comandantes in August 1981 he emphasized security issues and made little or no reference to Nicaragua's internal political practices."

Although democratic rhetoric within the foreign policy establishment was ostensibly meaningful, the Reagan administration's overall foreign policy focus was on security threats and relations with the Soviet Union (Haliday 1989). Therefore, as Carothers (1991, 103-104) argues,

> the Reagan administration gave only the crudest thought to the question of how democracy might one day come about in Nicaragua . . . [However] many U.S. officials involved in the Nicaragua policy from roughly 1984 on sincerely believed that the policy was increasing the chances of democracy. They were misguided in their understanding of how to promote democracy and were motivated primarily by anti-communism.

The 'democracy' position in the U.S. foreign policy establishment increased in importance over time, gaining more support under the Bush administration. The gradual change in relations with the Eastern bloc (including its consequent demise) and the pragmatic posture of the Bush team offered incentives to look for non-military options with regards to Nicaragua. The administration's strategy consisted of offering support to the Nicaraguan opposition while obtaining support from Congress. This strategy coincided with Daniel Ortega's decision to move the elections forward from November to February.

Shortly after George Bush was elected president he sought to reach a common ground with the U.S. Congress on Central America. Bush convinced House Speaker Jim Wright to work on creating a bipartisan policy toward Central America. As a result, on 24 March, 1989, the Bush administration and Congress reached a bipartisan accord that supported the Arias plan and also provided nearly $50 million in humanitarian assistance for the contras. The administration promised it would not request military aid before the Nicaraguan elections (Cocco 1989, 7). The February 1989 call for elections in Nicaragua helped bring about the agreement and allowed President Bush to concentrate on other international issues (Sojo 1991, 103).

The fact that President Bush supported a non-military option for Nicaragua does not mean the administration's intent to oust the Sandinistas had changed. Dislike for the Sandinistas was still fresh and intense. But the decision to support the election was a much-needed strategy if the administration was to succeed in having normal relations with Nicaragua. Acceptance of the election was combined with three other actions: creating a unified opposition, diplomatic pressure on the Sandinistas to respect the electoral process and retaining the contras in the background as a potential military option. Given the fragility of the Nicaraguan opposition, the Bush administration was compelled to support the contras if it hoped to abandon a military solution and remove the Sandinistas from power.

The existence of a strong and unified opposition was a critical issue in the electoral challenge to the FSLN. Opposition groups were considerably weakened by the political power of the Sandinistas, who intimidated and divided the different parties. Furthermore, because of the traditional patronage system in Nicaragua that depended on contests among local leaders and national elites, sustaining a unified position was difficult. The U.S. therefore played a critical role in forging an alliance among political parties that could face the Sandinistas.

After the 1987 peace agreement, the National Republican Institute for International Affairs (NRI) joined the National Democratic Institute for International Affairs (NDI) in launching a democratization program for Nicaragua (Robinson 1992, 48). The program consisted of establishing contacts with the Nicaraguan opposition and assessing its political strength for the election (then still scheduled for November 1990). It concluded that there was a need for further training of parties. In mid-1988, the State Department and the National Endowment for Democracy (NED) (a non-profit organization created by the U.S. government with the mission of promoting democracy), in close contact with the NDI and NRI, evaluated the future agenda of Nicaragua's internal opposition. The group agreed that training was important, but also stressed the need for a united opposition in Nicaragua, for which U.S. government support was important (Robinson 1992, 48-49).

When Ortega announced he would move the election date, the U.S. invested resources to create a unified opposition that could defeat the FSLN. Bringing the opposition together occurred at two levels or fronts. First, the U.S. attempted to unify the internal opposition parties, particularly those who had previously been aligned with each other. Second, it recognized that the opposition should contact the 'armed' opposition (contras) and establish alliances. To that effect, U.S. officials and NED representatives (to whom the U.S. government had entrusted the electoral training work in Nicaragua) encouraged a group of fourteen opposition parties known as the Nicaraguan Democratic Coordinating Committee (CDN) to forge a multiparty alliance for the February 1990 elections. The United States viewed this alliance as a 'third force' somewhere in between the contras and the Sandinistas (Cortes 1990, 291). In September 1989, the alliance came to be known as UNO. The U.S. commitment to support the opposition did not end with the facilitation of this opposition grouping. The U.S. also expressed its choice of Violetta Chamorro as UNO's presidential candidate; that she prevailed over other leading candidates reflected the U.S. influential role. Moreover, the Bush administration and Congress approved nine million dollars in funding for the election and various means of support for the opposition, while it continued pressuring the Sandinistas to hold to fair and free elections.

The NED was in charge of administering the funds. Five of the nine million dollars were intended directly to support UNO's electoral organization; the remaining four million would be used for monitoring the election. The NED distributed the funds to various non-profit organizations that used the monies to train opposition leaders in election issues, voter registration, democratic values, and campaign tactics, such as developing media advertisements. The table below shows the distribution of funds destined to support the Nicaraguan opposition. The NED tried to cover various political fronts; including labor unions, youth organizations, leadership, and the media.

Organizations like the NDI and NRI also received assistance from NED funding to train opposition leaders and citizens in voter registration and democratic election processes. Although the Bush administration argued that the financial support was a mechanism to "level the playing field;" the U.S. was openly supporting the opposition, intent to change the balance of power against the Sandinistas. This partnership was criticized by the Sandinistas as direct interference in Nicaraguan internal affairs. These financial contributions were mechanisms of control. During the elections the Bush administration continued to criticize the way the electoral process was handled. Vice-president Quayle called the voting a 'sham' while the State Department maintained constant criticism, "insisting that the FSLN raises grave questions as to whether there can be truly free and fair elections in Nicaragua" (Goshko and Kamen 1990).

Table 5.3 U.S. Funding for the Nicaraguan Elections

National Endowment for Democracy	$7,680,000
Unión Nicaragüense Opositora	$1,800,000
Supreme Electoral Council (SEC)	$1,800,000
Institute for Electoral Promotion and Training	$1,500,000
Vía Cívica	$220,000
Nicaraguan Labor Federation (distributed by the Free Trade Union Institute)	$493,000
Activities Consistent with Legislation	$970,000
Management, oversight	$897,000
Other funding	**$4,312,000**
Organization of American States	$3,000,000
President Carter's Council of Freely Elected Heads of State	$400,000
Inter-American Institute for Human Rights/CAPEL	$400,000
Center for Democracy	$250,000
Office of the Inspector General and one election expert	$180,000
Freedom House (money distributed to La Prensa newspaper, the Lawyers' Guild, the CDN)	$82,000
Total	**$11,999,200**

Source: Lopez-Pintor (1998) 41.

Openly supporting and funding the opposition, maintaining diplomatic pressures, and keeping the contras in the background were key factors that shaped the nature and outcome of the electoral and political process and even the outcome of the election. However, international involvement was not restricted to U.S. intervention. Other international actors were also active in promoting political change in Nicaragua.

International Monitoring

Daniel Ortega's call for international observers involved the entire electoral process, not only the voting itself. Monitoring the conduct of free and fair elections was a key objective of the international community. The UN and OAS, as the two international organizations given the status of official observer missions, were charged with verifying that the "electoral process has been governed by the strictest rules of equal access for all political parties" (UN 1991, 10). Their mandate provided for ascertaining whether participation was equal and fair, and investigating complaints, such as accusations of intimidation. The OAS and UN therefore exercised authority not only to ensure the success of the election, but also to shape the nature and outcome of the process as one that was fair and free.

The concept of 'fair and free elections' refers to specific issues of the electoral process. While fairness involves applying election rules in an unbiased manner, freedom applies to "elements relating to voters' opportunity to participate in the election without coercion or restrictions of any kind" (Elkit and Svenson 1997, 34). Elklit and Svenson (1997) note that an electoral process is composed of three phases; before, during, and after polling day. Monitors assess all these phases against the free and fair measurement of elections to produce a checklist of issues (see Table 5.4). Although this list is not comprehensive, it highlights a broad set of elements that monitors consider for evaluation. Evaluations vary somewhat depending on the specific conditions of each country. In the Nicaraguan case, major issues included freedom of speech and assembly and freedom from intimidation as well as the corresponding dimension of fairness or equity and impartiality.

In August 1989, the OAS and the UN worked in conjunction with the Carter Center to monitor the process. The OAS set up offices in the nine regions of the country. Each office was staffed by two people charged with hearing complaints about the elections. The organization's work concentrated on observing the registration process as well as looking at incidents of intimidation in various parts of the country (Wola 1989). By the end of the process it had received several hundred complaints. The most common included protests about the presence of armed men at voter registration places as well as intimidation of voters and other parties by Sandinista followers during campaign rallies. The OAS investigated the most relevant cases and presented its results to the Nicaraguan government. In most cases, the two sides were able to negotiate solutions.

Table 5.4 Issues Considered for Electoral Monitoring

Time Period	Dimension	
	"Free"	*"Fair"*
Before polling day	Freedom of movement	A transparent electoral process.
	Freedom of speech (for candidates, the media, voters, and others)	An election and an electoral system that grant no special privileges to any political party or social group.
	Freedom of assembly	Absence of impediments to inclusion in the electoral register.
	Freedom of association	Establishment of an independent and impartial election commission.
	Freedom from fear from the election and the electoral campaign	Impartial treatment of candidates by the police, the army, and the courts of law.
	Absence of impediments to standing for election	Equal opportunities for parties and independent candidates to stand for election.
	Equal and universal suffrage	Impartial voter-education programs. Orderly election campaign. Equal access to public media. Impartial allotment of public funds to parties. No misuse of government facilities for campaign purposes.
On polling day	Opportunity to participate in the election	Access to polling stations for parties, accredited local and international election observers, and the media; Secrecy of the ballot; Absence of intimidation of voters. Effective design of ballot papers. Proper ballot boxes; Proper counting procedure; treatment of void ballot papers; precautionary measures when transporting election materials. Impartial protection of polling stations.

After polling day	Legal avenues for complaint	Official and expeditious announcement of election results. Impartial treatment of any election complaints. Impartial reports on the election results by the media. Acceptance of the election results by everyone involved.

Source: Elkit and Svenson, Journal of Democracy: July 1997, v8, n3, p32.

The UN mandate to monitor the electoral process gave rise to the UN Verification Mission in Nicaragua (ONUVEN). ONUVEN opened offices in Managua and maintained close contact with the Supreme Electoral Council (SEC), the government institution that received complaints from the UN or the OAS. (Elliot Richardson was the UN envoy who led the mission.) ONUVEN evaluated voter registration procedures, media issues, election rules, and campaign activities (Richard and Booth 1995, 207). Like the OAS, ONUVEN carried out several investigations. Two of these were related to the opposition's free and fair access to the media. Although the government had established a TV channel for political parties to air their views, broadcasts did not reach the entire country (Wola November 1989, 3). When attempts were made to correct the problem, TV staff (who were Sandinista sympathizers) allegedly intimidated UNO members. In both cases the problems were solved after UN representatives dealt directly with Ortega and the head of the Supreme Electoral Council (Cortes 1990).

The OAS and the UN exerted a heavy influence on Nicaragua. Their reports were used as leverage to ensure the compliance of the Nicaraguan government with the electoral process. The two organizations released five reports each about the conduct of the elections. Each report gave the government good marks, an outcome that in large part reflected the organizations' influence. For the government, positive remarks about the election would give the international community more confidence in Nicaragua. Compliance with OAS and UN demands was therefore an important mechanism for gaining international support and legitimacy.

The Nicaraguan government's invitation of former president Jimmy Carter to monitor the election was a strategic decision that sought to provide credibility to the process. Carter and his Council of Freely-Elected Heads of Government were highly regarded by the Bush administration, the FSLN, and UNO. As Pastor (1992, 239) noted, Carter "received invitations from Ortega, UNO, and the SEC to observe the electoral process from 'beginning to end.'" Ortega promised Carter "unrestricted access to all aspects of the process." The members of the Carter team included thirty-five distinguished political personalities from the U.S. and the rest of the world. While the UN and OAS monitored the process throughout the country and dealt with local authorities, the Carter group dealt directly with Chamorro and Ortega. The group provided mediating mechanisms to solve disputes and sought to create a consensus about the conduct of the process. The group's role was important at a time when the polarization of society exhibited violent dimensions. After serious incidents of violence during campaign rallies, Carter was able to craft a joint agreement between Chamorro and Ortega on the conduct of campaign rallies. The Supreme Electoral Council adopted this agreement as a formal decree. As a result, cases of violence decreased substantially to the extent that the UN "reported that there were no more violent incidents, and UNO leaders attributed that fact to the decree" (Pastor 1992, 242).

In addition to the UN, the OAS, and the Carter group, other actors participated in the electoral process, either through support for particular political groups or by observing the whole electoral process. The Nicaraguan government also invited members of the international community as guests without authority over the conduct of the process. Some of these actors were the Friedrich Ebert and Konrad Adenauer Foundations, the American-based Hemisphere Initiatives, Oxfam-Canada, and the Washington Office on Latin America. In total, more than two thousand guest observers arrived in Nicaragua (Cortes 1990). To monitor the vote, the OAS sent 435 monitors to visit 3,064 voting sites (70% of the total), while the UN team deployed 237 observers who visited 2,155 sites (Wola 1989). In addition to the monitors, many other observers who had less authority influenced assessments of the outcome's legitimacy.

Election Outcome

Immediately preceding the elections and on the day itself, uncertainty persisted as to who the winner would be. The Sandinistas felt confident of a certain victory. This assessment was supported by opinion polls, which generally showed the Sandinistas with much more support than Chamorro. Polls from both left- and right-wing groups showed Ortega with at least 38% of the vote. However, the pollsters played down the number of undecided voters, who represented nearly 30% of the electorate in November 1989, three months before the election. By early February, this group had declined to 20%, with increasing support for Chamorro (Anderson 1995, 93). Those who indicated indecision may well have been concerned about the wisdom of openly expressing their political views; uncertainty therefore could have implied a tacit rejection of the Sandinistas. In a conversation with Sandinista government officials at the inauguration of Venezuelan President Carlos Andrés Pérez, Oscar Arias (interview 1997) recalls how he summarized the position of

Nicaragua's undecided voters: "The Nicaraguan people were afraid to express their opinions in a public opinion survey...[but] deep down the Nicaraguan people knew that a Sandinista victory implied the continuation of war. Thus they chose to elect doña Violeta (Translated by the author)."

By election day, uncertainty largely gave way to an increasingly tight race. As the voting count developed throughout the day, the results began to show a Sandinista defeat, increasing tension about the results. On the night of the election Daniel Ortega met with Carter, Richardson, and Baena Soares. Ortega conceded he was losing but did not yet accept defeat. The international representatives asserted that the count was definite. Carter persuaded Ortega of the importance of conceding defeat and reassured him of the accomplishments gained "from having defeated Somoza to holding a free election." The final results showed Ortega with nearly 41% of the vote against nearly 55% for Chamorro.

Ensuring success or shaping the outcome? Robinson (1992, 1996) argues that U.S. involvement in the election was an interventionist act that tilted the process against the Sandinistas. On the other hand, conservative U.S. groups believed the playing field was in the FSLN's favor, given the party's control of government and state resources. The international monitoring missions ultimately played a decisive role in Nicaragua's ability to reach free and fair electoral outcome. The OAS and UN exercised authority by conditioning their reports on government compliance with the electoral process. They succeeded in shaping a relatively clean election in the midst of heightened tensions.

Chapter 6

Democratization in the Aftermath of Civil War: Nicaragua in the 1990s

Nicaragua's Democratic Transition

Although democracy has been in the minds of Nicaraguans for many years, in practice it has been absent in their country's institutions due to prevailing authoritarian rule. Nicaragua's efforts to democratize took shape with the struggles to overthrow dictator Anastasio Somoza which culminated successfully in 1979 with the revolutionary upheaval led by the Sandinista movement which represented a hopeful change towards democratization. It attempted to redress the enormous inequality and poverty in the country with a range of programs to improve the lives of the poor. However, democratization was halted by two key obstacles. First, the Sandinista leaders rejected 'bourgeois' (liberal) democracy, and, shortly after they took power, the leaders began restricting liberties, such as rights of association, movement, and expression. Second, the United States treated the Nicaraguan revolution as an instance of communist expansionism, rejecting any opportunity for social reforms in the country. As a consequence a ten-year civil war ravaged the country in a tension between supporters of the Revolution and a coalition of anti-Sandinista groups formed by former members of the Somoza regime, middle-class sectors, peasants and other opposition groups. Moreover, the civil war was linked to growing internal opposition to the Sandinistas during the conflict.

As the previous chapter showed, after intense international efforts to end the civil war and bring democracy in the country, a regional peace agreement was signed that involved the cessation of hostilities between Sandinistas and contras. The peace agreement gradually moved the Nicaraguan conflict from the military to the political sector. In 1989, and within the context of peace negotiations, the Sandinista government agreed to hold elections in early 1990 as part of its compliance with the peace process (Cortes 1990). On February 25, 1990, the U.S.-supported National Opposition Union coalition (Unión Nacional Opositora; UNO) and its presidential candidate,

Violeta Barrios de Chamorro, the widow of a martyred newspaper editor, won the election.

A peaceful transfer was negotiated through the "Transition Protocol," an agreement by which the new Chamorro government committed itself not to remove General Humberto Ortega, brother of the now-defeated Sandinistas, as head of the Army. The transition process initiated in 1990 experienced four political transformations that characterized the country's democratization. These transformations were linked and influenced by international forces with the effort to support new or emerging non-traditional actors, fostering consensus, supplying material assistance and providing diplomatic or international recognition. First, power repositioning among leading elites culminated with the passing of Constitutional reforms and a new political configuration of national forces. Second, the power of the military gradually diminished. Third, society greatly enjoyed its ability to organize and participate in social and political events. Fourth, state reform sought to reduce the excessive interventionism of the state.

Power Repositioning

In an attempt to pursue national reconciliation, Chamorro's government eventually found itself in a tacit legislative coalition with the FSLN and a handful of UNO moderates. This coalition initially retained rather than surpassed a continued ideological polarization between Sandinistas and anti-Sandinistas inherited from the Somoza dictatorship and the civil war. The polarization revealed itself in a debate about the return of expropriated property by the Sanidinistas, the removal of Sandinista security officers, Humberto Ortega as head of the Army, and attention to demobilized combatants from the war. Because of these tensions the legislative body remained in chaos for nearly four years. Polarization also was observed in the form of civil disobedience and continued violence with disgruntled former Contras ("Recontras") and demobilized army personnel ("Recompas") taking up arms engaging in recurrent waves of violence that lasted more than four years. By 1995, however, after engaging in successive negotiations involving amnesty and material assistance to former contras, Chamorro had disarmed most of the rearmed groups and succeeded in decreasing civil disobedience (Table 6.1).

The international community in the form of training, food, and monetary incentives directly provided this assistance. Moreover, the prevailing legislative polarization gradually receded due to the emergence of moderate forces in the country composed of Christian Democrats and dissenting Sandinista groups who proposed important reforms to the Constitution and built a new national consensus.

Table 6.1 Civil Disobedience in Nicaragua, 1991-1995

Year	Land takeovers	Occupation of public Institutions	Riots	Public demonstrations	Labor strikes
1991	220	142	76	143	133
1992	162	174	124	116	85
1993	40	70	93	115	43
1994	36	60	76	92	23
1995	13	29	36	50	11

Source: Cuadra, Elvira, Andres Perez, and Angel Saldomado. *Orden social y gobernabilidad en Nicaragua 1990-1996* Managua: CRIES, 1998. p.65.

The reforms established among other points, that the president as well as his or her close relatives could not be re-elected; that presidential candidates had to win an election with at least 45% of the vote. If not, a second round would be held between the candidates in the first and second place. The reforms also increased independence of the judiciary from the executive. Chamorro opposed these reforms because they reduced the power of the president. However, after six months and in the context of international influence she passed the reforms. External actors, such as the Group of Friends of Nicaragua (made up of Spain, Mexico, Canada, Sweden, and Holland) had encouraged dialogue among the conflicting parties. Starting in March 1995, the Group sponsored a series of meetings to reduce the level of confrontation (CAR 1995, 5). Although these efforts facilitated the political debate, tensions lasted for more than four months due to Chamorro's continued opposition. This difficult period came to an end in June 1995 when she signed the laws.

Chamorro's decision to pass the legislation was a direct result of conditions imposed by Sweden as one of the members of the Group of Friends. Chamorro and her team were pressured to sign the reforms in exchange for securing increased economic assistance. In June 1995, Nicaragua was scheduled to negotiate international aid packages for 1996-97 in Paris. Eivor Halkjahr, Sweden's Ambassador in Nicaragua, explained that "without the Paris deadline, they [the government] would not have come to an agreement at this point" (Dye 1995, 6).

These Constitutional reforms represented a new political formula for the country, and also marked an emerging political configuration represented by two dominant political groups, the Sandinistas and the right, the latter mostly represented by the Liberals, and then by an array of small political groups who were unable to form a third force after the reforms.

Demilitarization

As part of a process of pacification that followed earlier peace agreements, Chamorro negotiated the formal demobilization of the Contras in June 1990 and cut the army from more than 80,000 to fewer than 15,000. But in 1994, after intense and critical negotiations, Chamorro was able to obtain the resignation of General Humberto Ortega, chief of the army since 1980, and drafted a military code that would impose regulations with regards to its relationship to civilian authorities. The removal, plus the code and the smaller army, signified greater civilian control over the military.

The resignation of Ortega and the change military code were largely influenced by the joint efforts of moderate groups and international actors. Recognizing the need to reform the Sandinista army was central to political change, and after conversations with Nicaraguan leaders, the U.S.'s National Democratic Institute established a civil-military relations program in 1992. The program consisted of analyzing the state of civil-military relations in the country, helping to create a consensus about improving those relations, and facilitating the creation of a Nicaraguan NGO working on civil-military relations, the Center for Strategic Studies. The initial NDI efforts on civil-military relations began with meetings with various influential sectors. NDI identified six concerns: national security policy was unclear, the Army was too large relative to national needs, the Army was partisan, there was no Ministry of Defense, the Army was too costly, and legislators lacked understanding of military issues.

In light of these weaknesses, NDI proposed a working agenda around five areas: establish dialogue among parties, debate changing the Army's name from the Sandinista People's Army to the Nicaraguan Army, train civilians in military issues, develop research centers, and encourage the idea of a Ministry of Defense. More broadly, NDI sought to sponsor a national dialogue on civil-military relations while simultaneously educating and training civilians in these same issues (NDI 1993). After a series of meetings between legislators, military, and the government sponsored by NDI, Humberto Ortega, then head of the Army, announced in one of these meetings that he was open to changing the name of the Sandinista Army, that he favored the establishment of a Defense Ministry, and that his departure "would conform with the stipulations set forth in a military law to be adopted by the National Assembly" (NDI 1995, 8). This law was later adopted in 1994. The facilitating efforts of the NDI eventually led to changes in the military: Ortega's resignation, and a military code which represented a consensus between the army and the Legislature and included issues that emerged from NDI activities.

The reduction of the army and the demobilization of former combatants as well as military personnel were also accomplished with the assistance of the international community, which provided financial resources to help the demobilized relocate into civilian life. Through the work of the International Commission of Support and Verification (CIAV), a commission set up to follow-up the demobilization process, CIAV monitored security threats against demobilized groups.

Pluralism

Demilitarizing the state was an important but not exclusive task in Nicaraguan democratization. Guaranteeing civil and political freedoms were other goals being pursued by political and social groups. Chamorro's government sought to guarantee the emergence of civic involvement in various spheres of national life with local and national leaders getting involved in organizing various civil society associations. Before 1990, Nicaraguan civil society included religious organizations (including charities), 'society' clubs and unions, although there were relatively few of the latter and they were mostly controlled by the Somoza dictatorship or Sandinista organizations. Since 1990, in contrast, Nicaragua has seen a dramatic growth in such elements of civil society as NGOs, unions, professional associations, and grassroots movements, many of them intertwined.

NGOs particular have become an important source of civic activism in the country. They are one of the few groups which encourage active participation in community issues as well as community voluntary work is encouraged. These organizations also play an important role in dealing with specific policy problems and function both as alternatives and complements to government work. Nearly two-thirds of NGOs in Nicaragua were created in the 1990s (particularly between 1990 and 1995), and 28% were created in the 1980s (See Table 6.2).[5]

Those organizations created in the 1990s are the product of a combination of three processes. First, with the Sandinistas' loss of power, a

---

[5] The information on NGOs is based on tabulation and analysis of information from the *Directorio ONG de Nicaragua 1996-1997*. Managua, CAPRI, 1997. This directory surveyed the characteristics of 239 NGOs considered by the authors as the country's most representative.

vacuum emerged among middle-rank civil servants who had occupied social policy positions in government during the 1980s and now found themselves without jobs. Many of these people decided to create non-profit organizations both to advance their policy positions as well as to find employment. In most cases, these local NGOs presented themselves as alternatives to the unpopular structural adjustment policies administered by the Nicaraguan government in compliance with international financial institutions' recommendations. Second, in the context of the globalization process, emerging international civil society organizations encouraged the formation of civil society in Nicaragua. Third, in the early stages of democratization, Nicaraguans felt encouraged to create spaces for social and political action in areas which they considered important. Intellectuals and other groups took the opportunity to organize into non-profit movements. The interplay of these three processes enriched the activism and work of NGOs.

Table 6.2 Founding Years of 239 NGOs in Nicaragua

Period	Percent
Before 1970	4.7
1970-1979	4.7
1980-1989	28.4
1990-1996	62.3
Total	100.0

Source: *Directorio ONG de Nicaragua 1996-1997*. Managua, CAPRI, 1997.

The progress of civil society has been supported by the work of external actors. Civic education in public schools, improved civil-military relations, attention to reforms within political parties, and regional autonomy were all important factors that contributed to continued democratization in Nicaragua. In many cases, a substantive international effort supported civil society and its projects. Donors helped create and strengthen the civil society sector by contracting with various non-government organizations to carry out democracy-building programs.

According to a study on democracy in Nicaragua (IDEA 1997), government donors funded more than one hundred democracy-building projects between 1993 and 1997 amounting to nearly two-hundred million dollars. These projects were managed by NGOs, various government agencies, and some international organizations. The implementation of these democracy programs created a web of interrelations between donors, international NGOs, local NGOs, and the state. For example, some NGO democracy projects funded and evaluated by AID established communication channels with government agencies and international NGOs, on occasion also funded by AID (USAID 1997).

Moreover, external actors' support for each of these organizations reflected their political and ideological positions with regard to the internal politics and tensions in the country. The U.S. government and NGOs tended to support programs that targeted liberal values and institutions, such as political parties, liberal education, civic-military relations, or human rights organizations of the right. In contrast, Scandinavian countries and organizations concentrated on aspects or factors that facilitated democracy through other means. They focused on organizations working on women's rights, popular education, or reconciliation through development programs.

A key issue with regards to international support is the impact it left on civil society and the country as a whole. In the first place, international cooperation has helped to strengthen this sector by providing material and financial assistance to these organizations to carry-out their goals. In the second place, Nicaraguan society has benefited directly from international cooperation as projects on civic education, women's rights, youth, and political party training, for example, helped to improve or educate society about its status in a democracy.

Chamorro's guarantees to peaceful national elections in 1996, and the transfer of power from one civilian government to another were significantly accomplished with the assistance of the international community. In October 1996 national elections were held with the FSLN and the new Liberal Alliance as the country's favorites. Daniel Ortega was the FSLN's presidential. The party's main campaign issues were aid to the poor, national unity and, in contrast to its historical stance, reconciliation with the United States. The Liberal Alliance, a coalition of three Liberal parties, was led by Arnoldo Alemán, previously mayor of Managua and allegedly a sympathizer of former dictator Anastasio Somoza. He and the alliance represented the political right in Nicaragua's convoluted political spectrum. He had long been an enemy of the Sandinista party and of Ortega in particular. Alemán's campaign raised the specter of a return to the Sandinista past, civil war, military service, and food rationing.

International assistance for the 1996 elections guaranteed the success of the political process and focused on three areas: a) assistance to the Supreme Electoral Council in achieving its objectives, b) monitoring the electoral process, and c) helping to create a national base of electoral observers. In the first case, the international community provided the SEC with more than fifteen million dollars to acquire equipment, to train and administer the registration as well as the election process. In the second case, backing local efforts to achieve a free and equal electoral process though domestic and international electoral monitoring was another key area of concern for international actors (Boneo 1997, 4). Concern for free and fair elections was evident in attempts to prevent fraud and, most important, to provide confidence among voters and parties that there was scrutiny of election conduct. The Organization of American States was the main organization observing the election. It was the only institution granted full status to monitor and supervise the electoral process. The electoral process was observed by over 1,200 international observers who represented an array of actors (governments, legislatures, political parties, local governments, social movements, and international NGOs). These actors both provided support to specific political groups (their local partners) and were concerned about the elections being well organized, free, and fair overall. Table 6.3 shows the distribution of international actors according to the status conferred on the different groups by the SEC. Four out of the five international organizations had representatives in Nicaragua (UN, OAS, the European Union, and the Central American Parliament). Sixteen (73%) out of 22 observing countries were based in Nicaragua; these 16 countries were half of all governments accredited in Nicaragua. Unlike governments and international organizations, social movements, international NGOs, political parties, and other community-based organizations that observed the elections mainly lacked a national affiliation or accreditation. In fact, only eight out of fifty-one international NGOs observing the elections were permanently based in Nicaragua. The rest were organizations with indirect interests or concerns in some of the Nicaraguan organizations.

    International actors also supported the formation of a national base of Nicaraguan election observers. The NDI played a key role in creating, developing, and training *Etica y Transparencia*, the first national election observer team in Nicaragua's political history (NDI 1996).

    When the SEC reported the official and final vote count one month later, declaring Alemán the winner, Daniel Ortega persisted in challenging the results of the elections. The Carter Center continued its involvement in the election and not only "concluded that Ortega's allegations of significant fraud were not proven" but former President Carter personally urged Ortega "to recognize the presidential results" (Carter Center 1996, 34). After international calls to recognize its defeat, the FSLN partially acknowledged the results and told Carter Center observers that the FSLN candidates "would take their seats as National Assembly members, mayors, city councilors, and Central American Parliament members" (Carter Center 1996, 35). The consistent international support of the validity of the election results, notwithstanding the technical errors, was key to granting legitimacy to the election and to give confidence to voters about their choice during an important transition period.

Table 6.3 Number of Observers by People and Groups

	Status	Main Observer	Guest Observer	Courtesy observers	Total
Governments	People		17	313	330
	Countries		8	14	22
Social movements, NGOs	People		183	467	650
	Groups		6	60	66 (51)*
International Organizations	People	117	109	4	230
	Groups	1	3	1	5
Total	People	117	322	784	1210
	Group	1	18	90	109

* 51 international NGOs. This table excludes 13 observers with no institutional affiliation. It also excludes electoral observers who were members of Central American Electoral Councils. Other actors involved in the election were Nicaraguans living abroad who gave almost total support to the Alemán campaign as a sign of opposition and challenge to the Sandinista party. Source: SEC 1996.

The vote consolidated key political allegiances and marked the division between traditional, pro-status quo groups (Liberals) and populist, pro-labor rights organizations (the Sandinistas). The preference for Liberals reflected traditionalism and conservative values, people's memories of life under the FSLN and public support for a free market economy.

State Reform

The political processes of the 1990s invited reform of the Nicaraguan state. This reform was a daunting (and still unfinished) task that involved overhauling the state apparatus; that is, the political institutions and the bureaucracy, as well as economic policy. These tasks required addressing problems that were causes of the revolution and the civil war, issues that emerged during the war, as well as issues of the war itself. The international community and the Chamorro government worked together to look for ways to do this work. However, mixed results were obtained including an increase in national poverty levels.

Institution-building in Nicaragua consists mainly of providing tools to create resources, retrain people, and reform institutions emerging from war conditions. Under the Sandinista government, the state apparatus grew considerably in size, ultimately becoming seven times larger than it was during

Somoza's last term (Table 6.4). As is observed from the table below, the number of ministries and autonomous agencies more than doubled, reaching a high of 285,000 public employees. The structure of this state was similar to that of a military command.

Table 6.4 Size of Bureaucracy in Nicaragua

Government	Ministries	Autonomous Agencies	Employees
Somoza	10	12	40,000
Ortega	19	400	285,000
Chamorro	15	44	95,000

Source: "Vice-Presidente Presentará Propuesta de Restructuración del Estado" NotiFax Managua: March 18, 1997.

Four important objectives were necessary to building institutional capacity for democratic governance. First, public employees had to be depoliticized and retrained. Second, the state needed to be demilitarized and made into a smaller civilian institution. Third, government had to become transparent and accountable. Fourth, state institutions had to be modernized.

With the peace settlement, it was necessary to challenge problems in the public sectors that went beyond material or resource constraints. The politization of the state, the lack of training and expertise in public service and the lax delivery of social goods were factors encouraging potential political tension. Most public employees were loyal to the Sandinistas and feared and disliked the new government. Depolitization of the ministries was necessary to reduce the tension between the incoming government and these employees. In reality, however, no measures were developed to prevent the potential tension. Changes were only symbolic: The government tried to neutralize the public service by changing names of buildings with Sandinista names and by requiring workers to wear civilian clothes instead of military uniforms (during the Sandinista regime, Nicaraguan employees in government offices wore military uniform regardless of their membership in the Army).

Relations in government offices remained tense for some time after the Sandinistas' 1990 electoral defeat. Public employees did not receive an education in public service, and obedience to civilian authority was never emphasized. Training in administration and service delivery was also neglected and contributed to maintaining internal polarization along political lines.

The size of the state bureaucracy gradually reduced as part of its demilitarization. State reform focused mainly on fulfilling structural adjustment of the economy. Yet, dismantling the large government created by the Sandinistas was an important part of creating a distinction between the ruling party and the state apparatus. The new government initiated a program to reduce the size of the state by cutting agencies and ministries and reducing the pool of employees to one-third its 1989 size. This project, however, contradicted the government's stated goal of increasing employment. Worsening unemployment in turn contributed to fueling tensions between Sandinistas, former contras wanting posts in government, and the Chamorro administration. Although economic support was provided to employees who were let go as part of restructuring the state, the amounts did not guarantee future employment in the private sector.

In the economic front, the Chamorro government had inherited a war-ravaged economy with a severely damaged infrastructure and productive sector, an impoverished society, and a prohibitive external debt. By 1990, Nicaragua's external debt amounted to $8 billion along with nearly $2 billion in unpaid interest. Indeed, interest alone Nicaragua owed the equivalent of one full year of its gross domestic product (Neira and Renzi 1996, 52). The value of exports, Nicaragua's main source of foreign currency, was the same as that of the 1960s. The population found itself in a severe economic depression, with very few employment opportunities and with the prospects of future layoffs. Under the influence of U.S. pressures thus the World Bank and International Monetary Fund, Chamorro's team chose to implement drastic neo-liberal economic policies. The main government's objective consisted of reactivating production by creating financial discipline, meeting international commitment, and trying to provide jobs to the population.

Chamorro's policy was able to stabilize the national currency, eliminate hyperinflation (which in the 1980s had reached five digits) and keep inflation in the single digits, and renegotiate various debt relief deals. By 1997 the country began to see some growth, although it was unable to recover to 1970's levels. As Figure 6.1 shows, per capita growth began to increase, although the adjustment policies had an adverse effect on the population, raising unemployment rate and decreasing income.

In combination with, and partly as a result of, the externally imposed fiscal discipline, political crises, stoppages, and strikes in the early 1990s, the economy was unable to reach normalcy, and thus remained (and remains) fragile. The very small growth rates did not translate into benefits for the majority of the population, of whom 80% live in poverty. Struggles for survival have become an everyday fact of economic life.

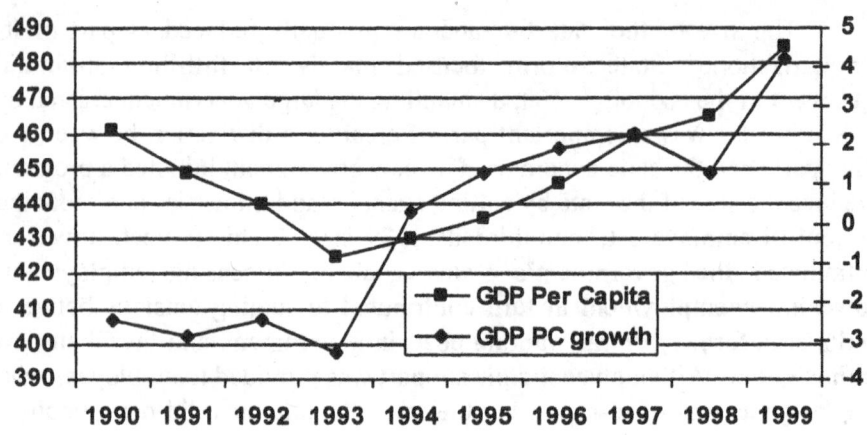

Figure 6.1 GDP Per Capita, 1988-1999

The Legacy of War and International Mobilization for Democracy

Democratic transition in the aftermath of a civil war faces specific constraints of a deeply divided society. The ruler's peace-maker profile and the rise of moderate forces facilitated a gradual transition chiefly aided by international assistance. The negotiated transition signed after the elections as well as the Constitutional Reforms passed in 1995 were key agreements that reflected a process that paved the way to continued democratization. These, however, were neither quick nor gradual negotiations; instead they were intermittent and highly conflictual. The rise of moderate groups amid polarization contributed, however, to the acceptance of negotiating a peaceful transition. The Constitutional Reforms represented a carefully organized political formula produced by moderate forces that addressed the interests of political elites. These moderate groups represented sectors of society that were gradually disengaging themselves from political polarization associated with the war.

In fact, the war left material and symbolic destruction in all sectors of society. Healing the wounds from the war required a comprehensive political, economic and a social reconstruction program which was missing from the outset. The war divided families and destroyed social linkages, as well as an already fragile and unequal economic infrastructure. The war wounds included continued scarcity and poverty, and a culture of violence which informed the lives of the youth and the national elites. Nicaragua's toll from the internal conflict of the 1980s has been estimated at $2.5 billion (two years of Nicaragua's GNP in 1994) and at least 35,000 deaths--the equivalent of 10 deaths per day and an annual loss of $270 million (Lake 1990, 111; Sivard 1995).[6] At the core of this culture of violence was a belief that solutions to problems or irreconcilable differences could only be found on a military battlefield.

Because underlying tensions between warring factions were still fresh and did not recede with the agreements on demobilization, the outbreak of war became certain. The relatively few working political institutions, i.e., the legislature and political parties, did not guarantee stability, nor did they have the material or human capacity to lift the country from political and ideological polarization. In addition, ten years of war created a large pool of mainly male combatants with no other skill and political culture than that of fighting wars. Upon their disbandment, demobilization, or discharge, their potential for violent behavior, at home or in the streets, was a disquieting reality.

Insecurity among former rebels and the Nicaraguan Army was thus constant. Former combatants felt threatened by the other side, and in many cases with just reason. In fact, rights violations against former rebels continued during the transition and demonstrated the fragility of the democratic transition. Thus, rearming illustrated the level of insecurity and a mechanism of protection at the same time.

However, Chamorro's government 'conflict-resolution' peacemaking profile helped ease the levels of insecurity as well as the political tensions in the country. The Chamorro government tried to pursue at least four goals during its administration: political reconciliation, disarming and downsizing the army, expanding civil liberties, and reforming the economy. The policy of national reconciliation particularly aimed at the Sandinistas, while unifying competing elites sufficiently to facilitate peace and governance. The policy of reconciliation defined the government as a 'peacemaker' in search of political stability. Reconciliation required a peaceful demobilization of former contras and reducing the role of the Army, while the provision of guarantees for civil and political liberties was key to democracy and social accord. Chamorro's support for rights secured the emergence of a civil society sector that did not exist before.

During the course of these events international actors involved themselves in the process as facilitators of consensus, mediators, and architects

---

[6] A more recent study values the damages at $5 billion. Alejandro Martínez Cuenca, *El comportamiento inversionista en Nicaragua,* N.13, Managua: FIDEG-Friedrich Ebert Stiftung, February 1994, p.8.

of democratic institutions by offering material resources and training. A large range of external actors participated in the democratization process in Nicaragua. Long-established democracies were the primary state actors promoting democracy abroad. Among these actors were France, the United States, Germany, and Spain and a number of less powerful and/or influential democratic states that have made democracy and human rights a major foreign policy issue. This latter group included countries like Canada, Sweden, Norway, Denmark, the Netherlands, and Costa Rica.

In addition to states, there were a large number of international non-governmental organizations involved in supporting democratic change. The National Democratic Institute, the Friedrich Ebert Foundation, the National Endowment for Democracy, and the Arias Foundation were some of the international NGOs operating in Nicaragua. Also, three key international organizations participated in the country's political process and in the democratization of the country. These were the UN, the OAS, and the EU. Table 6.5 lists some of the key actors participating in democratizing Nicaragua.

Table 6.5 International Actors in Nicaragua

Type	Actor
State	United States, Germany, Sweden, Canada, Costa Rica, Spain
International Organization	European Union, OAS, United Nations
Non-governmental	Friedrich Ebert Foundation, Konrad Adenauer, Carter Center, NDI, TechnoServe, Nicaraguan exiles

Moreover, international mobilization was present during different contexts. First, the international mobilization during the 1987 to 1989 peace negotiations and over the 1990 elections are explicit cases of international pressures to push forward a country to democratize. In these two instances, pressures not only originated from the United States but also from countries like Costa Rica and international organizations like the OAS. Second, international support for democracy by establishing democracy-building programs, strengthening the civil society sector, and improving civil-military relations during the Chamorro government were specific cases where actors were concerned with furthering the country's democratic institutions. Third, international stances against recalcitrant forces were observed in the case of the international position with regards to Constitutional Reforms. In that case, various states represented by the Group of Friends made clear that not passing the reforms constituted a threat to the democratization process and diminished the country's credibility. Fourth, the OAS support in the demobilization process of Nicaraguan rebels is an important example of promoting democracy through other means, security in this case. Relief efforts to help rebuild Nicaragua affected by hurricane Mitch in 1998 were directly linked to an international commitment to protect democracy, which culminated with substantial reconstruction assistance.

In this context various international mechanisms were employed. For example, geopolitics played a major role in defining a model of democracy for Nicaragua, characterized by the United States' control of its sphere of influence. Compliance with the dominant actor's claims was achieved by coercion or because the norms that underscore or justify that compliance have been internalized or recognized as legitimate by the country that is the object of control and international community. The use of control as a form of influence occurred specifically under the Reagan and Bush Administrations. In both the negotiation process and the 1990 elections in Nicaragua, the United States used its power position in the region to try to force a particular outcome in the Nicaraguan political process. Although the peace negotiations were not shaped according to U.S. plans, the 1990 elections were an effect of the U.S. control over the international agenda over Nicaragua.

Consent was also a strategy sought by international actors. The post-1990 period exhibited various instances of actors using consent as an influence. Not only did the U.S. change its policy influence from control to consent, but other actors such as international NGOs, Western European countries, and the OAS sought to promote democracy through consent. The international community's support of civil society is an important illustration of the mechanism of consent. Conditionality was also part of an interplay between international actors and domestic ones. As observed from the previous section a specific instance of conditionality in Nicaragua was the influence over the passing of the constitutional reforms. In that case continued foreign aid was conditioned to Chamorro signing the reforms. Finally open defiance to the regime was observed in Nicaragua. This was the case of Nicaraguans living in the United States. During the negotiation process and the 1996 election their actions were a direct response to challenges to the Sandinista political forces.

Table 6.6 summarizes the events and identifies the involvement of international mobilization in Nicaragua in areas that were critical for democratization. In most cases international influence used consent to bring democratic change in the country. More than one kind of actor implicated itself in promoting democracy and where actors identified particular issues as critical for the survival or advancement of democracy, such as the peace negotiations and the national elections in 1990 and 1996, more than one mechanism of influence was employed. In many cases, there was direct interplay between assistance programs and involvement in various events.

After the Constitutional Reforms' agreement, Chamorro told the Nicaraguan press: "Thank God I only have a year more in government . . . politics is a horrible thing" (quoted in Orozco 1995, 11). She matured politically as she learned the trade of government, though at a great cost. Chamorro inherited a devastated economy, political and ideological polarization, and an unfinished civil war. In six years of government substantive political change was achieved. The army was reduced in budget and personnel, a military code was drafted, and General Humberto Ortega stepped down as military head. Moreover, the recontras and other armed bands gradually began to disarm. The political standoff in the legislative assembly was solved through the passage of constitutional reforms, a growing civil society sector emerged and participated in the political process, and a second democratic election was successfully accomplished. In sum, the institutional framework for order and the rule of law in a democratic society was gradually taking shape. Comparing Larry Diamond's provision of prerequisites for a country to be democratic (that is, guarantees for universal suffrage, civilian control of the military, accountability of elected officials, pluralism, and the rule of law (Diamond 1999, 16-17)), Nicaragua meets most of his criteria. The country has guaranteed competition for power; non-elected officials such as the military no longer have domains of power reserved for their discretion; pluralism has evolved with the development of civil society; and individuals enjoy civil and political liberties. Despite meeting these criteria, the country is not totally democratic. Political institutions are in a process of formation, and security and accountability issues are not yet fully in place. However, since 1990 the country has continued to advance democracy undoing its legacy of civil war.

Table 6.6 Major Political Events in Nicaragua in the 1990s

Trend	Issue	Outcome	Date	Actors
Peace Negotiations	Negotiations to End War	Peace Agreements	87-89	USA/OAS/UN/CA/WE/CAN/SCAN/Exiles/INGOs
Power Repositioning	Polarization	Const. Agreement	94	USA, Sweden, Financial institutions
	Polarization	Military Code	94	NDI
	Polarization	Property Return		USA, Exiles,
	Polarization	Electoral Defeat	90	USA/OAS/UN/CA/WE/CAN/SCAN/Exiles
	Fragmentation	Multiparty Group Formation	94	
	Violence	Pacification Efforts	92-95	USA/OAS/UN/Exiles
Pluralization	Civil Society	Growth of Civic Organizations	90s	USA/OAS/UN/CA/WE/CAN/SCAN/INGOs
	Elections of 1996	First Democratic Transfer of Civilian Power by Another Civilian	96	USA/OAS/UN/CA/WE/CAN/SCAN/INGOs
	Political Culture	Emerging Civic Culture Among Students and Public	90s	USA/OAS/

Trend	Issue	Outcome	Date	Actors
	Local Development	Municipal Government	90s	USA/ Germany/ Friedrich Ebert Foundation
Demilitarization	Professionalize	Improve Status of Army		
	Demobilization	Manage the Process	91-95	OAS
	Army Restructuring	Reduce Size of Army	91-94	US
Reform	Bureaucratic Institutions	Modernize Public Sector and Political Institutions	91-97	USA/OAS/UN/CA/WE/CAN/SCAN/
	Economic Liberalization	Privatization	91-97	USA/OAS/UN/CA/WE/CAN/SCAN/IMF/WB

USA: United States; OAS: Organization of American States; UN: United Nations; CA: Central American countries; WE: Western European countries (Scandinavian countries excluded); CAN: Canada; SCAN: Scandinavian countries; exiles: Nicaraguan exile community in Miami; INGOs: International Non-governmental organizations; WB: World Bank; IMF: International Monetary Fund. *The ordering of the different mechanisms is not intentional, it reveals which mechanism was more influential.

Chapter 7
Limitations of the International Mobilization for Democracy

Limitations of International Mobilization

Is the existence of a norm of democracy promotion sufficient for democracy to prevail? This normative commitment, recent in origin, is one key factor explaining international mobilization to support democracy. Support for democracy, however, faces at least six limitations to the international support for democracy. First, while international actors mobilize to support other societies, democracy continues to be a domestic political process. Second, there is often a lack of continuity in support for democracy. Third, international actors face the constant challenge of moving from rhetoric to practice. Fourth, a weak organized internal opposition may impede efforts of international advocates of democracy. Fifth, a non-democracy's power position can affect support for democracy. Sixth, although there is a growing consensus about promoting democracy, international actors disagree as to the kind of democracy to establish.

The Domestic Nature of Democracy

Democracy is a political process that mostly occurs within territorial boundaries and it is in that particular space in which democratic entitlements are exercised or violated. In this context, foreign support toward democratization can help facilitate, accelerate, or build democratic roots only where there is an internal political process led by native masses, organized groups, and other political actors; it cannot create democracy from abroad. Despite attempts to make democracy global, the decision for foreign involvement is legitimate in so far as there is a broad internal demand for it. A democratic process is not only frustrated when external forces act without any consent from those domestic actors affected by non-democratic practices. Arguably, such actions are likely to threaten internal pressures for democracy.

In Central America, for example, the involvement and participation in domestic affairs by the CIA and the U.S. in the name of democracy strengthened the institutions that were causing repression and authoritarianism in the region. Even more damaging, American involvement may have lengthened, instead of accelerated, the process of democratization. What is important to understand is the fact that internal processes have their own dynamics which must largely determine the terrain in which international forces act.

Even when support has been received from abroad, a democratic process cannot permanently depend on the international dimension of democracy. When international actors seek to strengthen political institutions, they can do so within a time constraint, since the objective is to strengthen, not to become part of, the institution. In fact, when international support for democracy (liberalization, consolidation, or deepening) extends beyond its temporal condition and is unable to make democratic institutions self-sustainable, its permanence will only make those institutions or processes parasites of international support. Thus, democracy as an internal process can only be supported from abroad when such support accelerates democracy, without creating or re-creating dependency.

Continuity of Support

One of the common problems of international support has been its lack of continuity and consistency in democratization programs. While dominant international forces proclaim their commitment to democracy, they often restrict their actions to particular objectives or events. Once these goals are achieved, they withdraw support, thus creating inconsistent processes. Within this short-term perspective, one common problem is that international actors equate democracy with electoral suffrage or ending human rights abuses. Once international mobilization successfully promotes elections or stops abuses, the support is discontinued and dominant countries claim that the recipients of their aid are now democracies. The existence of formal elections and the reduction of the number of killings in a country have sufficed for outsiders like the United States to argue that a country is now democratic.

This crude assessment was a current theme during the Reagan administration. The administration's goals concentrated on pressuring undemocratic governments to hold elections, regardless of whether this was the most pressing aspect of democratic development. After the 1984 elections in El Salvador, for example, the United States labeled the country a democracy. Support for increased democratization was either withdrawn, slowed, or re-channeled to areas such as economic growth or military assistance. This caused unstable political processes, including an increase in repression, as a consequence of a "legitimate" regime's exercise of its right to preserve security in the country.

Lack of continuity is both a political issue and a policy problem. International actors are faced with multiple policy constraints when they carry out democracy-building programs. Some of these problems deal with obtaining continued funding, with providing appropriate design of programs, with producing accurate evaluation of a project and its impact, and with attending to local organizations' demands. A loss of funds, an inadequate program design, or an inaccurate evaluation can lead to the suspension of a democracy-building program. While continuity of support, diplomatic and material, is fundamental to guaranteeing democratization, it is not always easy to achieve.

Joel Barkan (1997, 389) addressed this point by advising that when support for democracy occurs by external actors,

> they must not become overly preoccupied with single events or activities, but remain sensitive to the fact that democratization requires the building of appropriate institutions of countervailing power and the establishment of a supportive political culture. Both are processes that occur over relatively long periods.

Thus, although free and fair elections are important, the benchmark for international continuity in democratic support must focus on guaranteeing its longevity and strength over time; that is, its physical institutionalization and symbolic and material impact.

From Rhetoric to Practice

Countries and other international actors need to mobilize with the consent of their internal constituencies (citizens or organizations of a state, or members of an organization). In the U.S., for example, the President and Congress may make opposing appeals of the public of the question of international democratic engagement. This limitation may have a positive feature if it prevents countries from acting undemocratically in the name of democracy. However, it affects the society in need of political change.

Weak Domestic Opposition

International support for democracy not only requires the presence of democratizing pressures in target countries; it also becomes more successful when it operates in an environment in which a society is building a democratic agenda and requires international experience to strengthen or carry it out.

When an organized domestic opposition is absent or lacks a well-articulated democratic strategy, the success of international mobilization is limited. This may explain why democratization occurred more quickly in El Salvador than in Nicaragua. In El Salvador, the 1991 peace agreement was more than a call to end the country's civil war. It implied a political agenda that contained guidelines for a new Salvadoran democratic process. The country engaged in a simultaneous set of reforms of the state and key spheres of society, including human rights, police and justice reform, national elections, social and economic forums, reconstruction plans, and monitoring of the pacification and democratization process. The fact that there was an agreed emphasis on creating a set of democratic structures encouraged the international community to expand its presence beyond promoting one or two elements of democratization.

In Nicaragua, in contrast, key issues that were essential to achieving democracy, such as protection for the rights of the demobilized and human rights monitoring, were not included in the 1989 agenda that called for elections and demobilization of the contras. These shortcomings delayed the democratization process substantially and prolonged instability. Ultimately, it was the painful experience of violence and the continued involvement and commitment of international actors who worked with various sectors of civil society that laid the groundwork for democracy in various areas.

Vulnerability

The strength or capacity of a state to resist international pressures to change is a major limitation in democracy promotion. Vulnerable countries, or not so powerful ones, have been subject to foreign intervention, political instability, and cultural penetration, making them more susceptible to external pressures to democratize than stronger ones. This can be observed in the case of Honduras, where the U.S. forced the military to restore civilian power and hold elections in 1981 (Kieh and Agbses 1993, 419). Honduras's ability to resist external pressure was limited due to its dependence on foreign military aid. In contrast, China is an undemocratic country whose political independence and economic bargaining power make it much less vulnerable to foreign pressure. However, this does not mean that efforts to democratize China are fruitless or that strong countries in general cannot be influenced.

What Kind of Democracy?

Although there is agreement as to the need to support democracy, there is not an agreed standard about how to promote it. Actors use various forms of democracy promotion and seek to emphasize one dimension of democracy over another. The U.S. has often equated democracy with universal suffrage, whereas international NGOs have stressed the importance of civil society. During moments of crisis, when international actors disagree over how to support democratic change due to contesting notions of democracy and the state of democracy, support decreases or delays efforts to improve political conditions.

Limitations of Democracy in Nicaragua

The combined effect of the limitations can have regressive effects on a country's democratization. Uncertainty is a prevailing variable that affects politics during fragile democratic transitions as in Nicaragua's. Given this frailty and the limitations mentioned above, authoritarian impasses or regressions can occur. In that case, the international community is faced with the challenge of intensifying its efforts to promote democracy.

After the 1996 election, Arnoldo Alemán became the new president and the FSLN remained the dominant opposition party. Alemán's victory consolidated key political allegiances and deepened a division between traditional, pro-status quo groups (Liberals) and populist, pro-labor rights organizations (the Sandinistas). Alemán's presidency adopted a personalistic and undemocratic ruling style. More significantly, democracy was strongly undermined by Alemán and the FSLN's negotiation of a political formula that would protects his influence in power after his term ended. The pact between these groups was designed to exclude other political forces from electoral competition or at least make participation extremely difficult.

Shortly after the electoral victory in 1996, Alemán encouraged Daniel Ortega to recognize defeat and move to establish a political agreement that would work for both *(La Prensa,* November 2000). By 1998, talks had moved onto the issue of achieving a political agreement through Constitutional reforms towards some form of power sharing scheme in government institutions, such as the Supreme Court, the Comptrollers Office and the Supreme Electoral Council (SEC). To the Sandinista faction supporting Daniel Ortega, this agreement represented an important stepping stone to achieve political power in the national election of November 2001. To Alemán supporters it represented a consolidation of their current grip on power as well as protection of the economic benefits they had achieved while in government. Formal negotiations took place in 1999 in which a number of issues were addressed, such as Alemán's demand for reelection, the division of Managua into three municipalities, which decreased its administrative and political influence, and the distribution between Liberals and Sandinistas of the Supreme Court, the Electoral Councils, and other key government institutions.

After eleven meetings, in August 1999 the two political forces had drafted a final version of the political agreement to be legalized through Constitutional reforms. Despite national oposition and rejection of the pact in public opinion and civil society, the reforms were published into law in the official government newspaper, *La Gaceta*, in January 2000. They included more than nine changes to the Constitution, including reforms to the Electoral Law. The electoral law established constraints on the formation of political parties. Two of the most damaging reforms were first, lowering from 45% to 40% the votes required to win an election in a first round, or to 35% if the leading party had a 5% lead over the other parties. Second, a minimum requirement of 3% of loyal endorsement from registered voters in order to participate in an election was established. The following tables show the reforms to the Constitution and electoral law.

Table 7.1 Reforms to the Constitution and Electoral Law
The Constitutional Reforms

DUAL NATIONALITY: The Constitution allowed the existence of dual nationality. This reform is a very important one as it provides incentives to Nicaraguans living abroad to retain or reaply for their Nicaraguan nationality while being citizens of another country. The intent or at least effect, was politically oriented, namely to legalize the status of a number of Alemán supporters who were U.S. citizens.
- LEGISLATIVE SEAT TO A PRESIDENT: This reform stipulates that after serving a term, the president automatically joins the Legislative Assembly. This change means that Alemán will continue to influence politics, now from Congress after 2001.
- SUPREME COURT OF JUSTICE MAGISTRATES: The number of its members increased from 12 to 16 members, dividing the positinos between the FSLN and Liberals.
- A BOARD IN THE COMPTROLLER'S OFFICE: The authority of the office changed from one person to a five member board, also composed ideologically.
- SUPREME ELECTORAL COUNCIL: The membership increased from five to seven members and three deputies. The formation followed an ideological divide.
- PRESIDENTIAL IMMUNITY: The number of votes required to remove the immunity of a president changed from a simple majority into a two thirds majority.
- ELECTORAL VICTORY: A candidate running for office can win an election with 40% of the vote (this was changed from 45%). However if a leading candidate has 35% of the votes and is 5% ahead of the candidate in the second place, then that candidate wins the election.

The Electoral Reforms
- PARTY FORMATION: In order for a political party to run, it must have 3% of support from those registered to vote. This equals about 73,000 registered voters.
- PARTY LOYALTY: Citizens can only express support for one political party and must do so with their signature. Supporting more than one party invalidates their endorsement.
- PARTY ORGANIZATIONAL STRUCTURE: A political party must have a complex structure comprised of a nine member national directorate, seven member departmental directorates,

and five representatives in each of the municipalities.
- LEGAL RECOGNITION: Political parties must achieve legal recognition at least one year before a national election, and six months before a municipal election. Opposition parties had only four months to achieve recognition to participate in the November 2000 municipal elections.
- NATIONAL PARTICIPATION: Parties must participate in all contests of a national election.
- PARTISANSHIP OF ELECTORAL AUTHORITIES: Electoral Authorities must be formed by the two major political parties. In case of an alliance they would be formed by the leading party of that alliance. The pact intended that these two parties should remain the FSLN and the PLC.
- MUNICIPAL ELECTIONS: Parties could be allowed to obtain 80% of the required signatures and representatives in 80% of municipalities and still be recognized as new parties.
- LOSS OF RECOGNITION: If the party earns less than 4% of votes in an election it has to apply again for recognition for the next election.
- POPULAR SUBSCRIPTION: Candidates have to be party members. Independents are not allowed.
- MUNICIPAL DIVISION: Managua was to be divided into three municipalities, resulting in gerrymandering.
- ALLIANCES: To form an alliance two requirements exist. All alliance member parties must obtain the 3% support from registered citizens, and the alliance must be lead by a political party, not by a new coalition.

Constraining Citizens and Eliminating Parties and Candidates

The Alemán government and the FSLN with Daniel Ortega as its leader, designed an almost perfect political formula that excludes other political actors from choosing the form of their participation in politics. Political parties were legally constrained through the reforms which eliminated their chances to run for government. The requirements were highly demanding and fragmentation followed as groups attempted to form coalitions and disagreements ensued. It also prevented the creation of regional parties or parties only interested in having legislative seats, not presidential candidates. Candidates wishing to participate in a contest were restricted in various ways. They could not run as independents or only for legislative seats.

After the reforms were implemented a political machine emerged designed to enforce a new *caudillo* system, organized through hierarchical settings, from top to bottom. The Supreme Court judges, Supreme Electoral Council (CSE) members, Bank Superintendency Chief, and Comptroller Office board now branded membership of two political flags, the FSLN and PLC. The previous heads of the Supreme Electoral Council, Rosa Marina Zelaya, and the Comptroller's Office, Agustin Jarquin, were pressured to resign from their positions. Jarquin suffered jail time for alleged fraud charges which in fact were Alemán's way of intimidating the controller's investigation of corruption activities of the president.[7] Mrs. Zelaya suggested there was political bias in the new membership. She commented that "the positions from the Electoral Affairs Division, and the General Directorate of Informatics represented the vertebral column of the elections, [and these are] positions held by Sandinista member Adonai Jiménez and Narciso Aguilera respectively" (*Inforpress* July 2000).

After the January implementation of the reforms, all political parties began to organize and form alliances to comply with the requirements. A significant number of small parties immediately decided not to participate, overwhelmed by the excessive demands placed by the CSE. However, at least seven political groups sought to engage in the political game. Some of these parties were the Movimiento Renovación Sandinista (MRS), Partido Liberal Independiente (PLI), Unión Social Cristiana (USC), Movimiento Democrático Nicaraguense (MDN), Pronal, Camino Cristiano, and Partido Conservador de Nicaragua (PCN). Attempts to form coalitions were part of the strategy, while the FSLN and PLC were hoping to have some of these parties excluded. To the Sandinista party it was important to have the MRS (and its alliance group, the Third Way) off the political landscape in order to run unchallenged as the party of the left. Alemán's party, the Liberal Constitutionalist Party (PLC), also wanted PLI and other smaller liberal groupings out of the electoral game. By February and March 2000, these political opposition parties sought to establish alliances as a third force to confront the two parties that had pacted with each other, abusing the Constitution and the legal framework to protect the status quo. Eight political groups agreed to form an implicit alliance supporting one party, the MDN, without formally declaring the alliance, thus avoiding the unrealistic quest of gathering the seventy-thousand and more signatures per party. However, the implicit alliance broke before it was formed; fifteen MDN leaders (some who were close friends of Alemán), fearing a Sandinista victory, endorsed the Conservative party and split from the movement (*Envio*, June 2000). The alliance, reorganized with five parties supporting the MRS, still moved forward and submitted 86,000 signatures to request legal representation to participate in the November 2000 municipal election. However, the Supreme Electoral Council rejected their petition. The Council eliminated 25,981 signatures because they appeared in other parties' lists; 31,829 were annulled for having invalid identification numbers; and

---

[7] In 1999 the Comptroller identified a number of anomalies and abuses of government resources on behalf of the president. The most public case was the use of resources to build infrastructure of the president's farm La Chilamapa, the construction of a special road leading to the president's home and a number of contracts with personal friends.

9,115 were annulled because they were said to appear twice in the list. Despite demands from the MRS to allow the party to compare the signatures with the registration polls, the SEC denied them that right without an explanation (*Envio*, July 2000). The refusal to comply with the demands from a political party may be linked to its inability to prove its verification work. In fact, according to the former director of the registrars office of the SEC, Maria Teresa Alemán, the institution does not have a system to guarantee the verificatoin and validity of signatures provided by registered voters (*Inforpress*, April 2000).

The MDN and MRS experience was only one case of the political maneuvering caused by the reforms emerging from the pact. The exclusion of Conservative Party's Pedro Solórzano from the electoral game was an example of the use of the formal institutions to inhibit political participation. Solórzano, a leader for the Conservative party was a favorite in Managua's municipality. Fearing a victory by Solórzano, the reforms redrew the municipal districts leaving this leader out of the Managua boundary. Solórzano, contested the boundary definitions and continued his move in the electoral campaign. However, in August after the Conservative Party submitted its request for participation fulfilling the requisites demanded by the SEC, Solórzano was prevented from participating under the Council's claim that the candidate had submitted two addresses, and then that he had reported no address, thus violating Art. 173 of the Electoral Law that demands that a candidate must have resided in the municipality at least two years (*Inforpress*, August 2000). Solórzano allowed William Báez to run for mayor instead. Another example of using the law to limit political participation occurred in the case of José Antonio Alvarado. Alvarado was a major supporter of Alemán and had functioned as Minister of Defense. However, he had grown critical of the way Alemán was conducting government and pacting, and was particularly critical of the proposal of having a Constituent Assembly instead of a national election. Following that plan would mean that Alemán had to remain in power for longer until the Assembly drafted a new Constitution. Alvarado was seeking to form a new political party, the Liberal Democratic Party. As a result of Alvarado's criticisms of Alemán and the attempt to form a new party, the Minister of Government, René Herrera, nullified Alvarado's nationality arguing that there were legal discrepancies that could not be reconciled. Although Alvarado had U.S. citizenship, in 1990 he had recovered Nicaraguan citizenship after applying for it. The government however nullified his nationality days after his new political allegiances were made public (*Inforpress*, May 2000).

Only four political parties (FSLN, PLC, PCN, and the Christian Way) ran for the 2000 municipal elections. One month prior to the deadline to form a political party for the national elections in 2001, a high degree of uncertainty prevailed in the country. Political divisions and intimidation plagued the country. Alemán used his power to discourage, weaken or intimidate his opponents, within or outside his ranks. In the end, despite a partial victory of the PLC with 94 of 151 municipalites won, the Sandinistas prevailed in some of the key Municipalities in the country: Managua, León, and Chinandega (and the Conservatives won Granada).

Table 7.1 Municipal Election: Votes by Party and Department

Department	PLC Votes and Municipalites Won		FSLN Votes and Municipalities Won		PCN Votes and Municipalities Won	
Boaco	22,069	5	11,139	0	10,569	1
Jinotega	45,987	7	30,558	0	6,694	0
Granada	18,650	2	18,466	1	14,242	1
Chontales	21,509	8	12,390	1	12,842	1
Raas	43,876	11	16,884	1	4,961	0
Nueva segovia	35,852	10	30,126	2	1,348	0
Madriz	25,457	7	23,193	2	940	0
Esteli	35,632	4	36,992	2	1,170	0
Carazo	23,457	6	21,810	2	6,543	0
Rio san juan	10,894	4	8,164	2	1,120	0
Masaya	34,320	6	30,610	3	7,552	0
Rivas	23,635	4	22,620	4	8,801	2
Matagalpa	67,717	9	53,807	4	15,758	0
Raan	19,672	3	17,280	4	5,263	0
Managua	128,056	3	180,018	6	88,511	0
Leon	46,588	3	56,486	7	4,980	0
Chinandega	33,494	2	48,278	11	12,551	0
TOTAL	636,865	94	618,821	52	203,845	5

An additional 5102 votes went to local parties from the autonomous regions. Camino Cristiano received 68,183 votes. Source: Supreme Electoral Council of Nicaragua, November 28th, 2000.

The 2001 Electoral Contest

The short-term outcome of the reforms and the municiple elections suggests that the FSLN and PLC succeeded in becoming the two dominant parties: a Sandinista group and the PLC rightist group with strong ideological links to the Somoza legacy. The November 2001 election was also framed by these contours. Although three major parties were participating in the contest, the FSLN with Daniel Ortega as its presidential candidate, the PLC with Enrique Bolaños, and the Conservative Party with Alberto Saborío, the Liberals and Sandinistas were the predominant groups.

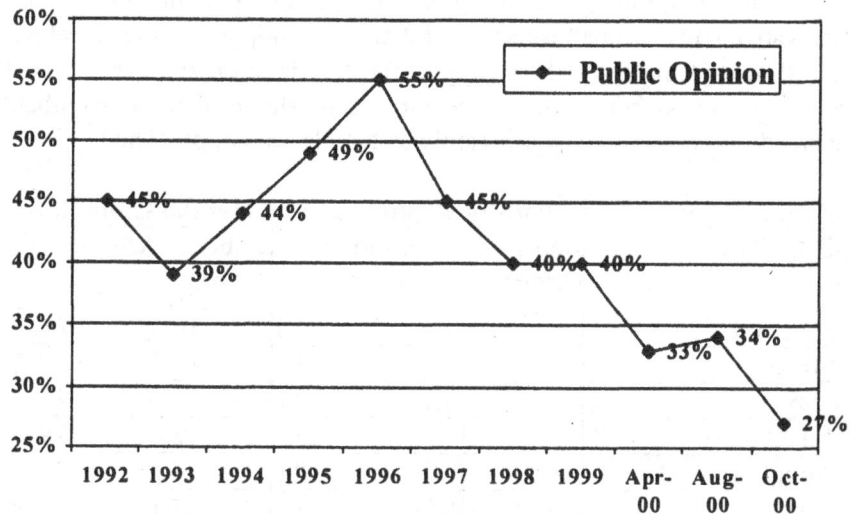

Figure 7.1 Decline of Arnoldo Alemán's Popularity

The election was one of the most contested campaigns in recent history. The two main candidates had very close margins of victory. Until October 2001 the opinion polls showed that the FSLN was ahead but only by 1% difference. Ortega had received the endorsement of Agustín Jarquin (the leader of the Social Christian Union) in exchange for the vice-presidency (Confidencial, September 2000). The FSLN party could count on at least 30% of popular support. The third party was weakened by internal fights and political intimidation by Alemán and could at best function as a 'spoiler', only attracting an insignificant percentage. The PLC had lost support due to Alemán's widespread corruption, reported almost daily in the national press. This problem combined with the fact that the PLC had difficulty raising electoral support because, unlike the FSLN, they could not count on a significant baseline constituency. Therefore the party's chances of wining were difficult but not impossible (La Prensa, October 2000).

Bolaños, a former member of COSEP, the private enterprise council, was Alemán's vice-president and had been highly criticized for supporting Alemán and not opposing corruption when he was in office. However, he enjoyed the support of the private sector and popular support grew as he distanced himself from Alemán.

The continued political pressure on the Conservative party eventually weakened its leaders. Tensions between traditionals and reformists in the Conservative party produced a split of the party which resulted in a decline of voter support. Ultimately the group was left in a very debilitated position. Conservative party sympathisers thus shifted their support to the Liberal party. The following table shows how support for the Liberal party increased at the expense of the conservatives. The table also shows that the number of undecided voters declined significantly as the election approached.

Table 7.2 Public Opinion Polls in Support of Presidential Candidates

Candidate	Daniel Ortega	Enrique Bolaños	Alberto Saborio*	Undecided
February	31.0	24.1	16.5	28.4
March	33.4	24.8	14.1	27.7
May 9	34.1	28.8	13.6	23.5
Jul 23 – 30	37.3	35.5	8.0	19.2
August 14 - 20	35.8	38.6	4.5	21.1
Sept 1 – 10	40.9	41.2	3.1	14.8
Sept 22 – 30	42.3	44.9	3.6	9.2

* The July poll shows the crisis of the Conservatives. *Confidencial*, Edición No. 244: Del 10 al 16 de Junio de 2001, Empate técnico Bolaños-Ortega, *La Prensa*, Jueves 9 de Agosto del 2001. Polls conducted by Borge & Asociados.

The scenario prior to the national election raised questions as to the implications of having a Sandinista victory tainted by an illegitimate pact.[8] The legacy of the FSLN continued to remain fresh in people's minds, and the public dislike of Daniel Ortega was very significant. Although he received support from a large segment of society, polls showed that 48% of the population would never vote for him (Borge 2001).

The end result of the election was an overwhelming victory for Enrique Bolaños who received 56% of the votes against 42% for the FSLN. His rupture from Alemán, the electoral support gained over time, people's fears

---

[8] A poll showed that Ortega had the lead in the election with 31%. Shortly after this poll, he endorsed the alliance with Christian Way. "Encuesta nacional de CINCO: ningún ganador a la vista" Confidencial, No. 233/ Del 18 al 24 de marzo de 2001.

about a Sandinista return, tipped the balance to Bolaños side. The Sandinista defeat demonstrated the party's inability to garner more than 40% vote for the third consecutive time (see Table 7.3).

Table 7.3 Nicaraguan Elections since 1990

Party	1990	1996	2001
FSLN	40.8	37.7	42.28
Other	5.3	11.15	1.41
Liberals*	53.9	51.06	56.3
FSLN defeat	13.1	13.36	14.02

Source: Supreme Electoral Council. * In 1990 the party running was the UNO.

The Role of the International Community and International Norms

The international community criticized the process and the outcome of the pact which set the stage for the elections. Countries and international NGOs committed to democratization expressed their disappointment at the pact, as well as to the intimidation of opponents. They supported the release of Agustin Jarquin from jail, for example. During the meetings with donor countries in the Consultative Group, Alemán was criticized for his handling of political affairs and was asked to hold a national dialogue (which he sponsored only to later disregard). Foreign assistance was reduced due to the lack of democratic governance. However, given the alliance between the two major political parties and the division among other opposition groups over a path of action, international actors were unable to further mobilize in order to prevent the pact.

One national and international concern during the campaign was the independence of the SEC. Given a tight electoral contest and a heavily biased electoral council there was uncertainty as to whether there would be a fair count of the votes. Prior to the election, analyst Carlos Fernando Chamorro argued that "it is not certain whether the Supreme Electoral Council will serve as an impartial and proficient arbitrator. It is certain that if the final result between two candidates is narrow, the Electoral Council, which is made up of three PLC magistrates, three FSLN, and a seventh that is pro-PLC, can potentially deadlock and divide along party lines on allegations of fraud from the losing candidate" (Latin America Advisor 2001). To that effect, the international community through election observers and international assistance, sought to ensure the independence and effectiveness of the council and prevent bias in the count. Thus, international actors monitored the Supreme Electoral Council's rejection of political parties and handling of the Conservative party. Instead actors such as the United States, the OAS, and members of the European Union invested efforts in monitoring the electoral process in an attempt to prevent violence or fraud.

International actors supported the technical capacity of the electoral council, and gave aid to a various national observing organizations. According to USAID, there were some 6,000 domestic observers. *Etica y Transparencia*, which was very successful in monitoring the 1996 election, was one major recipient of democracy aid. The table below shows the assistance received from various donor countries.

Table 7.4 Observation Assistance to *Etica y Transparencia*

Country	Observation of Election	Vote Quick Count
Norway, Finland, Sweden, Canada, Denmark, Holland	306,655	
USAID	134,989	69,290
Sweden		128,551
Germany	99,516	
Canada		31,750
Japan		52249
Total	541,160	281,840

Source: Etica y Transparencia, September 2001.

The United States in particular followed this election closely, and warned that it distrusted the FSLN. The U.S. government invested six million dollars in the Nicaraguan election, focusing on the efficiency of the SEC as well as in monitoring the electoral process and supporting civil society organizations (Johnson, 2001).

The politcal orientation of officials in the Bush Administration's staff raised concerns about reviving a Cold War approach with the Sandinistas. However, U.S. foreign policy showed contradicting commitments. The U.S.'s stated support for the democratic institutions was constrained and undermined by public statements of senior officials in the State Department who openly sided with Enrique Bolaños.

The electoral process represented a major step towards further democratization and the international community ensured the success of the election. However, supporting democratic governance continues to be a challenge to international actors. Consensus building and conditionality are tools to be used to stop the abuse of political authority and weakening of democratic institutions. Members of the OAS could make use of the Democratic Charter as a mechanism to hold a country and government accountable for the diminishment of democracy.

Globalization, Democracy and Sovereignty

Globalization is a process that has affected the traditional territorial political space and its associated claim to sovereignty. In the post-Cold War period, the promotion of democracy increased partly as a consequence of globalization and had direct implications on state sovereignty. This section analyzes the relationship between globalization, democracy, and sovereignty.

Globalization represents an increase and intensification of worldwide connectedness (and the consciousness of it) with some decline in the significance of territoriality and state structures. Anthony Giddens (1990, 64) defines globalization as "the intensification of worldwide social relations which link distant localities in such a way that local happenings are shaped by events occurring many miles away and vice versa." Following Giddens' definition, the absence or presence of democracy in one place has repercussions in other places. Furthermore, Held, McGrew, Goldblatt, and Perraton (1999, 484) speak of globalization in reference to four interrelated dimensions: scope (or 'stretching'), intensity (or 'deepening'), ease of connectivity (or 'speed') and impact (or effect of distant places in personal lives). In this context, the globalization of democracy involves the process of establishing its benefits in countries where it is absent, either through political opening--liberalization--or reform; making democracy stronger--democratic consolidation and deepening--where there are signs of weakness, as in cases of political violence, instability, or civil war, facilitating its change and creating consciousness in the public imagination about the state of democracy in the world.

When Giddens addresses the post-Cold War changes he argues that the development of modernity gave rise to globalization and in consequence to the treatment of democracy as an object of global attention. David Held further extended Giddens' notion of globalization to the experience of democracy Held (1996, 20) writes that "contemporary developments in the international order link people, communities and societies in highly complex ways and can, given the nature of modern communications, virtually annihilate distance and territorial boundaries as barriers to socio-economic activity." For Held, the key consequence of Globalization has been that "regional and global interconnectedness contests the traditional national resolutions of the key questions of democratic theory and practice." These national resolutions refer to the presumed symmetries between the nation state and decision-making acts within the state. The direct consequence of this process is the emergence of a number of 'internal' and 'external' disjunctures between states' claims to territorial authority and the practice of territorial control and sovereignty. Examples of such disjunctures are the penetrating power on sovereignty of international law, institutions, hegemony, global cultures, and the economy. The absence of freedom and democracy are triggering elements of international penetration. In Held's view, democratic political development is contingent on citizens' access to various sites of power in which political action occurs, namely, physical and social welfare, cultural and civic development, and economic and legal exercise. Furthermore, citizens from different countries working together within and across national borders have created regimes, institutions, and other organizations to 'cut across spatially delimited locales' to reinforce democracy.

If globalization has expanded the current international mobilization for democracy, what then are the implications for sovereignty? Sovereignty has traditionally meant that the state is subject to no other state and has full and exclusive powers within its jurisdiction, As Hinsley puts it, sovereignty means that "there is a final and absolute authority in the political community" and that "no final authority exists elsewhere" (cited in Held 1989, 215). However, globalization has led to a crisis of this traditional territorial nation-state construct we call sovereignty. Not only have democracies' roles been extended through attempts to make democracy global, but state autonomy has been challenged or changed by processes that have redefined the nature of sovereignty (Rosenau 1989,127).

On the one hand, the different responsibilities of nation-states have led them to abide by, and restrict their power to internationally recognized commitments as articulated in international laws, principles, and organizations. These commitments have at times subsumed the sovereignty rights of nations, both small and large, to the existence of higher authorities like the World Trade Organization, the International Monetary Fund, the World Bank, and other international organizations. International law, overall, has already constrained the exercise of sovereignty among states when they observe certain rights and duties.

On the other hand, the internationalization of the domestic life of the state and other actors has created a context of increased interdependence. This is observed, for example, in the process of international migration from the South to the North, in which people cross borders regardless of set boundaries. Saskia Sassen has addressed this issue, stressing the relationship between migration and global economics. She points out that when a state deals with immigrants, it "confronts the ascendant international human rights regime. Immigrants and refugees bring to the fore the tension between the protection of human rights and the protection of state sovereignty. This tension is particularly sharp in the case of undocumented immigrants, because their mere existence signifies the erosion of sovereignty" (Sassen 1996, 60). Another illustration of the internationalized life of states is observed in the number of international civil society movements that have a presence in various countries and claim certain rights. The nature of sovereignty is changing as a result of movements that are not necessarily restricted to the sphere of the state (Turner 1998).

More important and pertinent to the case of democratization is that the internal and external components of sovereignty have been conditioned to the presence of legitimate governments. David Held (1989, 215) observes that the internal aspect of sovereignty refers to the ability "of a political body to exercise 'supreme command' over a particular society," whereas the external dimension of sovereignty refers to the fact that "there is no final and absolute authority above and beyond the sovereign state." Thus states should be regarded as independent with regard to internal affairs and should be free to determine their choices.

The UN's recognition of the principle of non-intervention initially regarded these dimensions as indivisible. With the growing awareness of democracy at the end of the twentieth century, however, international actors sought to separate the two sides of sovereignty by stressing that its external dimension--that is, the principle that states are free to act in pursuit of their own affairs--needs to be reconciled with the existence of legitimate internal sovereign authority.

In this sense, international actors agree sovereignty is eroded not only when one state intervenes in the affairs of another, but also when a state violates human rights and denies democratic choices to its own citizens. This understanding has prompted the international community to react by condemning anti-democratic acts and mobilizing resources to build democracy. The prevalence of fundamental, universal values, such as democracy and human rights, precedes external sovereignty and makes its erosion unavoidable. The violating state or regime loses legitimacy, locally and internationally, when it abuses its authority. The efforts of the international community on behalf of democracy are legitimated in so far as its collective action in response to the abuse goes against perpetrators of violence. This mobilization of the international system toward the protection of democracy and human rights leads to what Gilbert calls "democratic internationalism," providing the necessary consensus that legitimizes foreign involvement (Gilbert 1992, 10). Actors stress that a regime that rules undemocratically is already eroding internal sovereignty and becomes subject to external scrutiny. When international actors mobilize their forces they restore sovereignty to its original source, the political community.

The European Union, for example, not only stresses that involvement is justified by international norms, but that these norms identify the principle of non-intervention as a relative one: "human rights are an important legitimate aspect of relations between States and no State can invoke the principle of non-interference as grounds for rejecting any manifestation of concern by other States at human rights violations" (European Union 1998). This latter point is also illustrated in the UN's Agenda for Democratization, which highlights the importance of democracy and its relationship to sovereignty.

> [With the expression] "We the Peoples of the United Nations," the founders invoked the most fundamental principle of democracy, rooting the sovereign authority of the Member States, and thus the legitimacy of the Organization which they were to compose, in the will of their peoples. The Charter offers a vision of democratic States and democracy among them that both derives from and aims to realize the founders' "faith in fundamental human rights, in the dignity and worth of the human person, in the equal rights of men and women and of nations large and small". Their commitment to democracy shows in the stated Purposes of the United Nations to promote respect for the principle of equal rights and self-determination of peoples and for human rights and fundamental freedoms for all without discrimination. . .
> The Universal Declaration of Human Rights, adopted unanimously by the General Assembly in 1948, elaborates upon this original commitment to democracy. The Universal Declaration proclaims the right of all individuals to take part in government, to have equal access to public service, and to vote and be elected. It further states that "the will of the people shall be the basis of authority of government," and that "this will shall be expressed in periodic and genuine elections which shall be by universal and equal suffrage and shall be held by secret vote or by equivalent free voting procedures". It also declares the right to equality before the law, to freedom of opinion and expression, and to freedom of peaceful assembly and association.
> Taken together, these three primary documents, the Charter of the United Nations, the Universal Declaration of Human Rights and the Declaration on the Granting of Independence to Colonial Countries and Peoples, provide a clear and solid foundation for a United Nations role and

responsibility in democratization.

The Universal Declaration of Democracy enacted by the Inter-Parliamentary Union (IPU) further strengthened this recognition of the UN. The IPU is an organization composed of legislators from more than one hundred countries and is recognized by the UN. The Union passed the declaration in 1997 in recognition of democracy as a legitimate right belonging to everyone. The first article of the declaration reads:

> Democracy is a universally recognized ideal as well as a goal, which is based on common values shared by peoples throughout the world community irrespective of cultural, political, social and economic differences. It is thus a basic right of citizenship to be exercised under conditions of freedom, equality, transparency and responsibility, with the due respect for the plurality of views, and in interest of the polity.

The international community has thus articulated its commitment to extending and strengthening efforts in support of democracy by following normative mandates. The most pressing challenge pertains to its capacity to enforce its norms and give to them durability through its institutionalization.

Bibliography

This section contains government documents, books, journal articles, newspapers, Internet material. Some sources were obtained through the Internet. Whenever this was the case, the citation contains the URL (web address) "◇", and followed in parentheses the date when the site was accessed.

Acevedo, Domingo, and Claudio Grossman. (1996), "The Organization of American States and the Protection of Democracy." *Beyond Sovereignty: Collectively Defending Democracy in the Americas*, Tom Farer. Baltimore: The Johns Hopkins University Press.

Aguilera, Gabriel Abelardo Morales y. Carlos Sojo. (1991), *Centro America: de Reagan a Bush*. San Jose: FLACSO.

AID. (1997), *USAID Fiscal Year 1997 Congressional Presentation*. Washington, DC: USAID; <http://www.info.usaid.gov/pubs/ cp97/countries/ni.htm> (03-13-99).

Alvarez Montalvan, Emilio. (1994), *Las Fuerzas Armadas en Nicaragua*. Managua: Edicion Jorge Eduardo Arellano.

Americas Watch. (1991), *Fitful Peace: Human Rights and Reconciliation in Nicaragua*. New York: Human Rights Watch.

Angell, Alan. (1996), "International Support fo rthe Chilean Opposition, 1973-1989: Political Parties and the Role of Exiles", *The International Dimensions of Democratization*, Lawrence Whitehead. Oxford: Oxford University Press.

ANPDH. (1992), *Información Esquematizada sobre la Desmovilizados de la Resistencia Nicaragüense Muertos*. Managua: ANPDH.

___. (1992), *Planteamientos de ANPDH sobre la reforma policial*. Managua.

___. (1994), *Situación de los derechos humanos, Nicaragua 1994*. Managua.

___. (1995), *Situación de los derechos humanos, Nicaragua 1995*. Managua.

___. (1996), "El ejercito de Nicaragua y los derechos humanos", *Reflexión* 5, no. 20 February.

___. (1996), *El Poder Judicial*. Managua: ANPDH, May.

___. (1996), "La desigualdad jurídica en la nueva de ley de la policía nacional", *Reflexión* 5, no. 23

___. (1996), *La indefensión en los procesos criminales*. Managua: ANPDH, October.

ANPDH. (1996), "La Policia Nacional y el Respeto a los Derechos Humanos", *Reflexión* 5, no. 21 March.

___. (1996), *Los Grupos Armados en Nicaragua*. Managua: ANPDH, March.

ANPDH. (1996), *Situacion de los Derechos Humanos en Nicaragua, enero-junio, 1996*. Managua: ANPDH.

___. (1996), *Situacion de los derechos humanos, Nicaragua 1996*. Managua:

Bibliography

ANPDH.
Apodaca, Clair, and Michael Stoll. (1999), "United States Human Rights Policy and Foreign Assistance", *International Studies Quarterly* 43, no. 1 March: 185-198.
Archibugi, Daniele, and David Held. (1995), *Cosmopolitan Democracy: an Agenda for a New World Order*. UK: Polity Press.
Arias, Oscar. (1997), interview by author, Tape recording, San Jose, Costa Rica, July-August.
Arnson, Cynthia J. (1989), *Crossroads: congress, the Reagan administration and Central America*. New York: Pantheon Books.
Baker, Pauline. (1996), "Conflict Resolution Versus Democratic Governance", Chester Fen Osler Hampson with Pamela Aall Crocker. Washington: United States Institute of Peace.
Ball, Nicole. (1996), "The Challenge of Rebuilding War-Torn Societies", Chester Fen Osler Hampson with Pamela Aall Crocker. Washington: United States Institute of Peace.
___. (1997), *Making Peace Work: the role of the international development community*. Washington DC: ODC.
Barkan, Joel D. (1997), "Can established democracies nurture democracy abroad?" *Democracy's Victory and Crisis*, Axel Hadenius. Cambridge: Cambridge University Press.
Barricada. (1987), "Contadora makes historic Central American Tour", *Barricada internacional*, 29 January: pp. 1-6.
Bendaña, Alejandro. (1992) *La firma de Esquipulas II: una perspectiva sandinista*. San José: Fundación Arias para la Paz y el Progreso Humano.
___. (1996), *Power Lines: U.S. domination in the New World Order*. New York: Olive Branch Press.
Bennett, Philip. (1990), "Ortega pledges party will block major changes", *The Boston Globe*, National/Foreign, 28 February: 1.
Berryman, Phillip. (1994), *Stubborn Hope: Religion, Politics and Revolution in Nicaragua*. New York: Orbis Books.
Bloomfiled, Lincoln P. and Allen Moulton. (1997), *Managing International Conflict: from theory to policy*. New York: St. Martin.
Bobbio, Norberto. (1984), *El Futuro de la Democracia*. Mexico: FCE.
___. (1996), "El Futuro de la Democracia", 2nd. ed. Mexico: FCE.
Boneo, Horacio. (1997), *Evaluación del Impacto de la Asistencia External en el Proceso Electoral Nicaragüense*. Sweden: International IDEA, October.
Booth, John A. (1998), "The Somoza Regime in Nicaragua", *Sultanistic Regimes*, 134-152. eds. H. D. Chehabi, and Juan Linz. Baltimore: Johns Hopkins University Press.
Booth, John. (1992), *Understanding Central America*. Boulder: Westview Press.

Booth, Ken, and Steve Smith. (1995), *International Relations Theory Today*. Pennsylvania: The Pennsylvania University Press.
Borge, Victor (2001), "Milagro Electoral de Enrique Bolaños" interview with, of

Borge y Asociados Polling firm August 9.

Boutros-Ghali, Boutros. (1992), *An agenda for Peace: Preventive diplomacy, peacemaking and peace-keeping*. New York: United Nations.

Bratton, Michael and Nicolas van de Walle. (1997), *Democratic Experiments in Africa: regime transitions in comparative perspective*, Cambridge: Cambridge University Press.

Bretherton, Charlotte and Geoffrey Ponton. (1996), *Global Politics: an introduction.* Oxford: Blackwell Publications.

Brockett, Charles D.(1991), *Land, Power and Poverty: Agrarian Transformation and Political Conflict in Central America*, revised ed. Boulder: Westview Press.

Brown, Michael E. (1996), *The International Dimensions of Internal Conflict.* Cambridge: CSIA.

Burgenthal, Thomas. (1992), "The Helsinki Process: Birth of a Human Rights System", in *Human Rights in the World Community: Issues and Action*, Richard Pierre Claude, and Burn H. Weston. 2nd. ed. Pennsylvania: The University of Pennsylvania Press.

___. (1998), *International Human Rights* , St. Paul : West Publishing Co.

___. (1997), "The Normative and Institutional Evolution of International Human Rights", *Human Rights Quarterly* 19: 703-723.

Burnell, Peter. (2000), Democracy Assistance: International Cooperation for Democratization. London: Frank Cass Publishers.

Butler, Judy, David Dye, Jack Spence, and George Vickers. (1996), *Democracy and Its Discontents: Nicaraguans Face the Election*, Cambridge, Massachussets: Hemisphere Initiatives, 1 October.

Cajina, Roberto. (1996), *Transición Política y Reconversión Militar en Nicaragua, 1990-1995*, Managua: CRIES.

Caminos, Hugo, and Roberto Lavalle. (1989), "New Departures in the Exercise of the Inherent Powers by the UN and OAS Secretaries-General: The Central American Situation", *The American Journal of International Law* 83, no. 2: 395-402.

CAR . (1995), "Constitutional Stand-Off Continues", *Central America Report* , April: 5.

Carothers, Thomas. (1994), "Democracy and Human Rights: policy allies or rivals?" *Washington Quarterly* 17, no. 3 June: 109-121.

___. (1991), *In the name of Democracy: U.S. Policy Toward Latin America in the Reagan Years*. Berkeley: University of California Press.

___ (1999), *Aiding Democracy Abroad: The Learning Curve* Washington, DC: Carnegie Endowment for International Peace.

___. (1997), "The Observers Observed", *Journal of Democracy* 8, no. 3: 17-31. Carter Center. (1996), *The Observation of the 1996 Nicaraguan Elections*. Atlanta, Georgia: The Carter Center of Emory University.

Carothers, Thomas. (1990), *Observing Nicaragua's Elections, 1989-1990*. Atlanta, Georgia: The Carter Center of Emory University.

___. (1995), *Report on a Property Issues Conference*. Atlanta, Georgia: The Carter Center of Emory University, 13 July.

Bibliography

Casper, Gretchen, and Michelle Taylor. (1996), *Negotiating Democracy: transitions from authoritarian rule*, Pittsburgh: University of Pittsburgh Press.
Castro, Vanesa and Gary Prevost. (1992), *The 1990 Elections in Nicaragua and their Aftermath*. Lanham, MD: Rowman and Littlefield.
Cavallini, Isabel . (1989), "End of the road for the contras", *Barricada Internacional*, 19 August: pp. 11-14.
"Chamorro rules but Sandinistas retain power", (1990), *ISLA*, July: 95.
Chamorro, Violeta. (1996), *Dreams of the Heart: the authobiography of President Violeta Barrios de Chamorro of Nicaragua*, New York: Simon & Schuster.
Chehabi, H. D., and Juan Linz, ed. (1998) *Sultanistic Regimes*, Baltimore: Johns Hopkins University Press.
Child, Jack. (1992), *The Central American peace process, 1983-1991*. Boulder: Lynne Rienner Publishers.
CIAV. (1993), *Comisión Tripartita: Memoria de Trabajo, 1990-1993*. Managua: OEA.
___. (1995), *Comisión Tripartita: Cuarto Informe de Avance*. Managua, Nicaragua: OEA, September.
___. *La Mision*. Managua: CIAV-OEA, undated.
___. (1996), *Nicaragua: Desplazados de post-guerra en las zonas rurales, Enero 1995 - Junio 1996*. Managua: OEA-Programa de Seguimiento y Verificación (PSV).
___. (1996), *Proceso de paz en Nicaragua: Verificación de Derechos Humanos, Resolucion Pacifica de Conflictos y Construcción de la Paz*. Managua: OEA.
Clark, Ann Marie, (2001), *Diplomacy of Conscience: Amnesty International and Changing Human Rights Norms* Princeton: Princeton University Press.
Clarke, Gerard. (1998), "Non-governmental Organizations (NGOs) and Politics in the Developing World", *Political Studies* XLVI: 36-52.
Clements, Kevin. (1994), *Building International Community: cooperating for peace*. Australia: Allen and Unwin.
Coatsworth, John H. (1994), *Central America and the United States*. New York: Twayne Publishers.
Cocco, Marie . (1989), "A bipartisan blockbuster; Bush, Congress agree to non-military contra aid and peace plan", *Newsday*, 25 March: 7.
Conroy, Michael E. (1990), *The political economy of the 1990 Nicaraguan elections*. Austin: Texas Papers on Latin America.
Cortell, Andrew P., and Jr James W. Davis. (1996), "How do international norms matter: the domestic impact of international rules and norms", *International Studies Quarterly* 40: 451-478.
Cortez Dominguez, Guillermo. (1990), *La Lucha por el Poder, reves electoral Sandinista*. Managua: Editorial Vanguardia.
Cranna, Michael. (1994), *The True Cost of Conflict*. New York : The New Press.
Crocker, Chester and Fen Osler Hampson. (1996), *Managing Global Chaos: sources of and responses to international conflict*. Washington, DC: US Institute of Peace.

Cuadra, Elvira, Andres Perez Baltodano, and Angel Saldomado. (1998), *Orden Social y Gobernabilidad en Nicaragua 1990-1996*, Managua: CRIES.

Dade County. (1995), *Hispanics in Dade County 1990.* Miami: Office of Latin Affairs, Dade County Office.

Dalpino, Catharin E. (2000), *Deferring Democracy: Promoting Openness in Authoritarian Regimes*. Washington, DC: Brookings Institution Press.

Diamond, Larry. (1999), *Developing Democracy: Towards Consolidation*. Baltimore: The Johns Hopkins University Press.

___. (1996), "Democracy in Latin America: Degrees, Illusions and Directions for Consolidation", in *Beyond Sovereignty: Collectively Defending Democracy in the Americas*, 52-104. edited by Tom Farer. Baltimore: The Johns Hopkins University Press.

___. (1997), "Promoting Democracy in the 1990s: actors, instruments and issues", *Democracy's Victory and Crisis*, Axel Hadenius. Cambridge: Cambridge University Press.

Diamond, Larry, and Marc Plattner. (1999), "Election Watch", *Journal of Democracy* 1-10, no. various issues: end of journal; <http://jhupress.jhu.edu/journals/journal-of-democracy/election-watch/> (02-02-1999).

Dominguez, Jorge. (1998), *International Security and Democracy: Latin America and the Caribbean in the Post-Cold War Era*. Pittsburgh: University of Pittsburgh Press.

Donnelly, Jack. (1998), "Human rights: a new standard of cilization?" *International Affairs* 74: 1-24.

Doyle, Michael Ian Johnstone and Robert C. Orr. (1997), *Keeping the peace: Multidimensional UN operations in Cambodia and El Salvador*. Cambridge: Cambridge University Press.

Dunkerly, James. (1994), *The pacification of Central America*. London: Verso.

Dunkerley, James. (1988), *Power in the Isthmus: A Political History of Modern Central America*, London: Verso.

Dunn, John. (1996), "The dilemma of humanitarian intervention: the executive power of the Law of Nature, after God", *The History of Political Theory and Other Essays*, John Dunn. Cambridge: Cambridge University Press.

Duran, Esperanza. (1988), "Western Europe's role in the Central American crisis: possibilities and limitations", *Central America: crisis and possibilities*, Roberto Garcia. Stockholm: Institute of Latin American Studies.

Dye, David. (1995), "A Chamorro Dynasty Dashed In Deal Struck in Nicaragua", *Christian Science Monitor*, 20 June: 6.

Dye, David.(1993), "Nicaragua Opens Era of Reform", *Christian Science Monitor*, 14 December : 6.

Dye, David R., Judith Butler, Deena Abu-Lughod, Jack Spence, and with George Vickers. (1995), *Contesting Everything, Winning Nothing: the search for consensus in Nicaragua, 1990-1995*, Cambridge : Massachussets, November.

Edwards, David. (1992), *Ethics, efficiency, and reflective practice*. Austin:

University of Texas, Unpublished.
Elklit, Jorgen, and Palle Svensson. (1997), "What Makes Elections Free and Fair", *Journal of Democracy* 83, no. 3: 32-44.
Envio (2000), "A Society Scandalized" Managua: June.
Envio (2000), "The Air is Thick with Electoral Fraud" Managua: July.
Envio. (1990), "The War Ends-where is peace?" *Envio* 9, no. 108 July: pp. 38-48.
EU. (1998), *Building Europe Together: HUMAN RIGHTS, DEMOCRACY AND FUNDAMENTAL FREEDOMS*. Brussels: <http://europa.eu.int/en/comm/dg10/build/en/democ.htm>(01-11-1998), February 1998.
Everingham, Mark. (1996), *Revolution and the Multiclass Coalition in Nicaragua*, Pittsburgh: University of Pittsburgh Press.
Farer, Tom, ed. (1996), *Beyond Sovereignty: Collectively Defending Democracy in the Americas*, Baltimore: The Johns Hopkins University Press.
Featherstone, Scott Lash and Roland Robertson. (1995), *Global Modernities*. London: SAGE Publishers.
FIDEG. (1994), *El Observador Economico*, Managua, Nicaragua: Fundacion Internacional para el Desafio Economico Global.
Finnemore, Martha. (1996), *National Interests in International Society*. Ithaca: Cornell University Press.
Finnemore, Martha, and Kathryn Sikkink. (1998), "International Norm Dynamics and Political Change", *International Organization* 52, no. 4: 887-917.
Florini, Ann. (1996), "The Evolution of International Norms", *International Studies Quarterly* 40 (1996): 363-389.
Fox, Gregory H. (1992), "National Sovereignty Revisited: perspectives on the emerging norm of democracy in international law", *American Society of International Law Proceedings* (1992).
Fox, Gregory H. and Brad R. Roth, (2000), *Democratic Governance and International Law*. Cambridge University Press, 2000.
Fox, Gregory, and Georg Nolte. (1995), "Intolerant Democracies", *Harvard International Law Journal* 36, no. 1 December.
Franck, Thomas. (1992), "The Emerging Right to Democratic Governance", *The American Journal of International Law* 86: 46-91.
Franck, Thomas (1995), *Fairness in International Law and Institutions*. Oxford: Clarendon Press.
Frost, Mervyn. (1996), *Ethics in International Relations: A Constitutive Theory*. Cambridge: Cambridge University Press.
Fukuyama, Francis. (1991), "The End of History?" *Taking Sides: Clashing Views on Controversial Issues in World Politics*, John T. Rourke. Connecticut: The Duskin Publishing Group, Inc.
Galtung, Johan. (1990), "Cultural Violence", *Journal of Peace Research* 27, no. 3: 291-305.
Gamble, Andrew. (1993), "Shaping a New World Order: political capacities and policy challenges", *Government and Opposition* 28, no. 3: 323-338.
Gastrow, Peter. (1995), *Bargaining for Peace: South Africa and the National Peace Accord*. Washington DC: US Institute of Peace.

Geoffrey Pridham, Eric Herring, and George Sanford. (1994),*Building Democracy?: the international dimension of democratisation in Eastern Europe*. London: Leicester University Press.

Giddens, Anthony. (1990), *The Consequences of Modernity*. Stanford: Stanford University Press.

Gilbert, Alan. (1992), "Must global politics constrain democracy?" *Political Theory* 20, no. 1

Gills, Barry, Joel Rocamora, and Richard Wilson. (1994), *Low Intensity Democracy in the New World Order*. London: Pluto Press.

Goertz, Gary. (1994), *Contexts of International Politics*. Cambridge: Cambridge University Press.

Goldstein, Judith. (1993), *Ideas, Interests, and American Trade Policy*. Ithaca: Cornell University Press.

Goldstein, Judith, and Robert Keohane. (1993), *Ideas and Foreign Policy: Beliefs, Institutions and Political Change*. Ithaca: Cornell University Press.

Gomariz, Enrique. (1988), *Balance de una Esperanza: Esquipulas II un año después*. San Jose: FLACSO.

Goodfellow, William and James Morrell. (1992), "Esquipulas: Politicians in Command", *Political parties and democracy in Central America*, 267-286. William and James Morrell Goodfellow. Boulder: Westview Press.

Goshko, John M., and Al Kamen. (1990), "U.S. Accused of Overstating Managua Election Offenses", *Washington Post*, A, 25 January: 29.

Grabendorff, Wolf. (1992), "The Party Internationals and Democracy in Central America", *Political Parties and Democracy in Central America*, Louis Goodman. Boulder: Westview Press.

Grugel, Jean. (1996), "Supporting Democratisation: A European View", *European Review of Latin American and Caribbean Studies* 60, no. June: 87-104.

Gruson, Lindsey. (1990), "In Contra Stronghold, Fear Also Goes to Polls", *The New York Times*, A, 1 25 February: 6.

Gurr, Ted Robert. (1993), *Minorities at Risk: a global view of ethnopolitical conflicts*. Washington, DC: US Institute of Peace.

Gutman, Roy. (1988), *Banana Diplomacy: The Making of American Policy in Nicaragua: 1981-1987*, New York: Simon and Schuster.

Hadenius, Axel, and Fredrik Uggla. (1996), "Making Civil Society Work, Promoting Demcoratic Development: What Can States and Donors Do?" *World Development* 24, no. 10: 1621-1639.

Halliday, Fred. (1989), *From Kabul to Managua: Soviet-American Relations in the 1980's*. New York: Pantheon Books.

Halperin, Morton H., and Kristen Lomasney. (1998), "Guaranteeing Democracy: A review of the record", *Journal of Democracy* 9, no. 2: 134-147.

Hampson, Fen Olser. (1996), *Nurturing Peace: why peace settlements succeed or fail*. Washington, DC: US Institute of Peace.

Hannum, Hurst. (1996), "Rethinking Self-determination", in *International Human Rights in Context: law, politics, morals*, Henry J. Steiner, and Philip Alston. Oxford: Oxford University Press.

Bibliography

Harris, Peter, and Ben Reilly. (1998), *Democracy and Deep Rooted Conflict: Options for Negotiators*. Sweden: Institute for Democracy and Electoral Assistance.

Harris, Richard, and Carlos M. Vilas, ed. (1985), *La Revolución en Nicaragua: Liberación Nacional, Democracia Popular y Transformación Económica*, México: ERA.

Hasenclever, Andreas, Peter Mayer, and Volker Rittberger. (1997), *Theories of International Regimes*. Cambridge: Cambridge University Press.

Hauchler, Ingomar, and Paul M. Kennedy. (1994), *Global Trends: The World Almanac of Development and Peace*. New York: The Continuum Publishing Company.

Held, David. (1989), *Political Theory and the Modern State*. Stanford: Stanford University Press.

Held, David. (1995), *Democracy and the Global Order: from the Modern State to Cosmopolitan Governance*. Stanford: Stanford University Press.

___. (1996), *Models of Democracy*, California: Stanford University Press, 2nd. ed..

Held, David and Anthony McGrew. (1992), "Globalization and the Liberal Democratic State", *Government and Opposition* 28, no. 2: 261-285.

Herrera Zuniga, Rene. (1994), *Nicargua, el derrumbe negociado: los avatares de un cambio de régimen*. México : El Colegio de México.

___. (1991), *Relaciones Internacionales y Poder Político en Nicaragua*. México : El Colegio de México.

Holiday, David and William Stanley. (1993), "Building Peace: preliminary lessons from El Salvador", *Journal of International Affairs* 46, no. 2: pp. 415-438.

Huntington, Samuel. (1991), *The Third Wave*. Oklahoma: Oklahoma University Press.

Hurrell, Andrew. (1996), "The International Dimensions of Democratization in Latin America: the case of Brazil", *The International Dimensions of Democratization*, Lawrence Whitehead. Oxford: Oxford University Press.

IDB. (2000), *Nicaragua. Basic Socio-Economic Data*. Statistics and Quantitative Analysis Unit. http://www.iadb.org/int/sta/ENGLISH/brptnet/brptframe_eng.htm (11-01-1998)

IDEA. (1997), *Mapeo de Proyectos Dirigidos al Fortalecimiento de la Demcoracia en Nicaragua, 1993-1997*, Sweden: IDEA unpublished.

Iliff, Laurence . (1993), "Guerrilla Rumors Tied to Attack on Mexico Peasants", *Houston Chronicle*, 3 October: 34A.

Inforpress Centroamericana (2000), "Desconfianza impera en el ámbito pre-electoral" 28 de Julio.

Inforpress Centroamericana (2000), "Indeciso proceso electoral en marcha" Guatemala: 28 de Abril .

Inforpress Centroamericana (2000), "Entre Partidos te veas: candente ambiente pre electoral" Guatemala: 18 de Agosto.

Inforpress Centroamericana (2000), "Renuncia evidencia lucha por el poder" Guatemala: 26 de Mayo.

Ionescu, Ghita. (1991), *Leadership in an Interdependent World: the statesmanship*

of Adenauer, De Gaulle, Thatcher, Reagan and Gorbachev. London: Longman.
IPU. (1997), *Universal Declaration of Democracy*. Inter-Parliamentary Union.
IRELA. (1996), *Elecciones en Nicargua: Consolidación de la Democracia?* Madrid: Instituto de Relaciones Europeo-Latinoamericanas.
ISLA. (1990), "Disarmed and disillusioned, the contras arm again", August: 599.
ISLA, (1990), "In contra stronghold, fear also goes", February: 810.
ISLA, (1990), "Ortega says he'll defend social changes", February: 827.
Jackson, Robert. (1990), *Quasi-States: Sovereignty, International Relations, and the Third World*, Cambridge: Cambridge University Press.
___. (1993), "The Weight of Ideas in Decolonization: Normative Change in International Relations", *Ideas and Foreign Policy: Beliefs, Institutions and Political Change*, Judith Goldstein, and Robert Keohane. Ithaca: Cornell University Press.
___. (2000), *The Global Covenant : Human Conduct in a World of States*, Oxford: Oxford University Press.
Jaime, Felipe . (1995), "Constitutional Reforms and Changes in the Military", *InterPress Service/Spanish (PeaceNet)*, 1 January.
Jason, Karen J. (1992), "The Role of Non-governmental Organizations in International Electoral Observing", *International Law and Politics* 24: 1794-1667.
Jelin, Elizabeth, and Eric Hershberg, ed. (1996), *Constructing Democracy: Human Rights, Citizenship and Society in Latin America*, Boulder: Westview University Press.
Johnson, James Turner. (1995), "International Law and the Peaceful Resolution of Interstate Conflicts", *Beyond Confrontation....*, 155-178. John Vasquez. Ann Arbor: The University of Michigan Press.
Johnson, Stephen. (2001), *Nicaraguan Elections Demand More Effective U.S. Support* Washington, DC: The Heritage Foundation. September 10.
Johnson, Tim . (1995), "Nicaraguan Lawmakers Want No More Dynasties", *Miami Herald*, A, 2 March: 16.
Johnstone, Ian. (1995), *Rights and Reconciliation: UN Strategies in El Salvador*. Boulder: Lynne Rienner.
Kaballo, Sidgi. (1995), "Human Rights and Democratization in Africa", *Political Studies* XLIII: 189-203.
Kamrava, Mehran. (1993), *Politics and Society in the Third World*, London: Routledge.
Karatnycky, Adrian. (1998), "Freedom in a democratic age", *Freedom in the World 1997 to 1998*, New York: Freedom House.
Keane, John. (1988), *Civil society and the state : new European perspectives*. London: Verso.
Keck, Margaret, and Kathryin Sikkink. (1998), *Activists Beyond Borders: advocacy networks in international politics*, Ithaca: Cornell University Press.
Kieh, George Klay, and Pita Ogaba Agbese. (1993), "From Politics back to the barracks in Nigeria: a theoretical exploration", *Journal of Peace Research*

30, no. 4: 409-426.
Kinzer, Stephen. *Blood of brothers: life and war in Nicaragua*. New York: Doubleday, 1992.
Klare, Michael. (1989), *Low Intensity Conflict*. New York: Pantheon Books.
Klare, Michael, and Peter Kornbluh, ed. (1987), *Low-Intensity Warfare: Counterinsurgency, Proinsurgency and Antiterrorism in the Eighties.*, New York: Pantheon Books.
Klotz, Audie. (1995), *Norms in International Relations: The Struggle against Apartheid*. Ithaca: Cornell University Press.
Korey, William. (1998), *NGOs and the Universal Declaration of Human Rights*. New York: St. Martin's Press.
Kornbluh, Peter. (1987), *The Price of Intervention: Reagan's Wars Against the Sandinistas*, Washington DC: Institute for Policy Studies.
Kratochwill, Friedrich and Yosef Lapid. (1996) *The Return of Culture and Identity in IR Theory*. Boulder: Lynne Rienner.
Kratochwill, Friedrich, and John Gerard Ruggie. (1994), "International Organization: A State of the Art on an Art of the State", in *International Organization: A Reader*, Friedrich Kratochwill, and Edward D. Mansfield. New York: HarperCollins College Publishers.
Kubalkova, Vendulka, Nicholas Onuf, and Paul Kowert.(1998), *International Relations in a Constructed World*. New York: M.E. Sharpe.
Kumar, Krishna, ed. (1998), *Postconflict elections, democratization and international assistance*, Boulder: Lynne Rienner.
Kumar, Krishna ed. (1997), *Rebuilding Societies After Civil War: Critical Roles for International Assistance*. Boulder: Lynne Rienner.
La Prensa (1996), "Alemán llama a Ortega a concertar pacto de gobernabilidad en Nicaragua", Noviembre 23, Honduras.
La Prensa (2000), "Presidente Alemán admite desgaste", Managua, Jueves 19 de Octubre.
La Prensa (2001), "Renuncian candidatos conservadores" Martes 17 de Julio.
Lake, Anthony. (1990), *After the wars: reconstruction in Afghanistan, Indochina, Central America, Southern Africa and the Horn of Africa*. New Brunswick: Transaction Publishers.
Landau, Saul. (1993), *The Guerrilla Wars of Central America: Nicaragua, El Salvador and Guatemala*. New York: St. Martin's Press.
Landsberg, Chris. (1994), *"Directing from the stalls?: The international community and the South African negotiation forum"*, Johannesburg, SA: CPS International Relations Series.
___. (1994), *Isolation, Permanent Neutrality, Non-alignment, or internationalism: towards a post-apartheid policy orientation.* , Johannesburg, SA: CPS International Relations Series, February.
Latin America Advisor, (2001), Thursday, August 9, Washington, DC.
Lederach, Jean Paul. (1997), *Building Peace: Sustainable Reconciliation in Divided Societies*. Washington, DC: US Institute of Peace.
Legro, Jeffrey W. (1997), "Which norms matter? Revisiting the "failure" of

internationalism", *International Organization* 51, no. 1 December: 31-63.
Leiken, Robert. (1984), *Central America: Anatomy of Conflict*. New York: Pergamon Press.
Leogrande, William M. (1991), "From Reagan to Bush: the transition in US policy towards Central America", *Journal of Latin American Studies* 22: pp. 595-621.
Li, Chien Pin. (1993), "The Effectiveness of Sanction Linkages: Issues and Actors", *International Studies Quarterly* 37: 349-370.
Licklider, Roy. (1993), *Negotiated settlements in civil wars since 1945*. New Brunswick: unplublished.
___. (1993), *Stopping the Killing: How civil wars end*. New York: New York University Press.
Linklater, Andrew. (1998), *The Transformation of Political Community*. Columbia: University of South Carolina Press.
Linz, Juan, and Alfred Stepan. (1996), *Problems of Democratic Transition and Consolidation: Southern Europe, South America, and Post- Communist Europe*, Baltimore: Johns Hopkins University Press.
Lopez Castellanos, Nayar. (1996), *La Ruptura del Frente Sandinista*, Mexico: Plaza y Valdes.
Lopez-Pintor, Rafael. (1998), *Postconflict elections, democratization and international assistance*, ed. Krishna Kumar. Boulder: Lynne Rienner.
Lowenthal, Abraham F. (1991), *Exporting Democracy: The United States and Latin America-Themes and Issues*. Maryland: Johns Hopkins University Press.
Lutz, Ellen L. (1997), "Strengthening the Core Values in the Americas: Regional Commitment to Democracy and the Protection of Human Rights", *Houston Journal of International Law* 19: 643-657.
Macdonald, Laura. (1997), *Supporting Civil Society: The Political Role of Non-Governmental Organizations in Central America*. New York: St Martin's Press.
Maingot, Anthony P. (1996), "Haiti: Sovereign Consent versus State- Centric Sovereignty", *Beyond Sovereignty: Collectively Defending Democracy in the Americas*, Tom Farer. Baltimore: The Johns Hopkins University Press.
Mainwairing, Scott, Guillermo O'Donnell, and J. Samuel Valenzuela, ed. (1992), *Issues in Democratic Consolidation: the new South American democracies in comparative perspectives*, Notre Dame, Indiana: University of Notre Dame Press.
Mannin, Mike. (1996), "Global Issues and the Challenge to Democratic Politics", *Global Politics: an introduction*, 220-246. Charlotte and Geoffrey Ponton Bretherton. Oxford: Blackwell Publications.
Marks, Susan. (1997), "The "Emerging Norm": Conceptualizing "Democratic Governance"", *ASIL Proceedings*
Marshall, Monty G. and Keith Jaggers, *POLITY IV Project: Political Regime Characteristics and Transitions, 1800-2000*.
http://www.bsos.umd.edu/cidcm/inscr/polity/index.htm
Marti Puig, Salvador. (1997), *La Revolución Enredada: Nicaragua 1977-1996*,

Madrid: Los Libros de la Catarata.

Martínez Cuenca, Alejandro. (1994), *El comportamiento inversionista en Nicaragua*, Managua: FIDEG-Friedrich Ebert Stiftung, February.

Martz, John D. (1995), "The Championing of Demcracy Abroad: Lessons from Latin America", in *United States Policy in Latin America*, ed. John Martz. Nebraska: University of Nebraska Press.

Mattiace, Shannan and Roderic Ai Camp. (1996), "Democracy and Development: An Overview", in *Democracy in Latin America: Patterns and Cycles*, ed. Roderic Ai Camp. Delaware: Scholarly Resources Inc.

Mawlawi, Farouk. (1993), "New conflicts, new challenges: the evolving role for non-governmental actors", *Journal of International Affairs* 46, no. 2 December: 391-413.

McGarry, John, and Brendan O'Leary. (1993), *The Politics of Ethnic Conflict Regulation*. New York: Routledge.

Mendez Asension, Luis. (1986), *Contadora: Las Cuentas de la Diplomacia*, Mexico: Plaza y Valdes.

Ministerio de Cooperación Externa. (1996), *Cooperación de los Organismos No-Gubernamentales Internacionales a Nicaragua, 1990-1996*. Managua: MCE.

___. (1996), *Memoria de la Cooperación Externa, 1990-1996*. Managua: MCE.

___. (1996), *Negociaciones de deuda externa: 1990-1996*. Managua: MCE.

Moreno, Dario. (1994), *The Struggle for Peace in Central America*. Florida: Florida International University Press.

___. (1990), *U.S. Policy in Central America: the Endless Debate*, Miami: Florida International University Press.

Mouffe, Chantal, ed. (1992), *Dimensions of Radical Democracy: Pluralism, Citizenship, Community*, London: Verso.

NDI. (1995), *Civil-Military Relations in Nicaragua*. Washington, DC: NDI, June.

___. (1995), *NDI Manual: Manual para la Observación Nacional de Elecciones*. Washington, DC: NDI.

___. (1993), *Relaciones Civiles-Militares en Nicaragua: informe de una delegación del NDI*. Washington, DC: NDI, March.

NDI. (1996), *Voter Registration and Domestic Election Observation in Nicargua*. Washington, DC: NDI, <http://www.ndi.org/lacivnet/ nicjul96.htm> (01-11-1998), July.

NED. (1998), *Organizations*. Washington, DC: National Endowment for Democracy, http://www.ned.org/page_4/orginfo.html (01-11-1998), November.

Neira Cuadra, Oscar. (1996), *ESAF: condicionalidad y deuda, nada por nada o nada por menos?* Managua: CRIES.

Norsworthy, Kent. (1990), *Nicaragua: a country guide*. Albuquerque: Inter Hemispheric Education Resource Center.

Norsworthy, Kent, and William I. Robinson. (1987), *David and Goliath : the U.S. war against Nicaragua*. New York: Monthly Review Press.

North, Liisa and Tim Draimin. (1990), "The decay of the security regime in Central America", *International Journal* 45: pp. 224- 257.

Nuñez, Orlando, ed. (1995), *La Guerra y el Campesinado en Nicaragua*, Managua: CIPRES.
OAS. (1996), *Electoral observation in Nicaragua, 1996*. Washington, DC: Organization of American States, internet download <http://www.oas.org/EN/PROG/UPD/dwnld/nicarage.exe> (01-11-1998).
____. (2001), *Inter-American Democratic Charter*. Washington, DC OAS, September.
____. (1990), *Report of the Secretary General on Observation of the Passage of the Electoral and Mass Media Laws of Nicaragua*. Washington, DC: OAS, August.
____. (1991), *Third Report on the Observation of the Nicaraguan Electoral Process*. Washington, DC: OAS, 4 November.
O'Donnell, Guillermo. (1994), "Delegative Democracy", *Journal of Democracy* 5, no. 1 January: 55-69.
O'Donnell, Guillermo, Philippe Schmitter, and Lawrence Whitehead, ed. (1986), *Transitions from Authoritarian Rule: Latin America*, Baltimore: Johns Hopkins University Press.
Opazo Bernales, Andres y. Rodrigo Fernandez V. (1990), *Esquipulas II: Una Tarea Pendiente*. San Jose: EDUCA.
Orentlicher, Diane F. (1992), "The United States Commitment to International Human Rights", in *Human Rights in the World Community: Issues and Action*, Richard Pierre Claude, and Burn H. Weston. 2nd. ed. Pennsylvania: The University of Pennsylvania Press.
Orozco, Manuel. (1995), "Aiding Central America: Official Development Assistance to Central America", *Relaciones Internacionales* 49, no. 3.
____. (1995), *Freedom in One Country? The international dimensions of democracy*. Johannesburg: Centre for Policy Studies.
____. (2001), "The Peril of Democracy in Nicaragua: Institutional Constraints to Political Competition and Citizenship Participation" in *Entrecaminos* Spring, Washington.
Orozco, Manuel. (1999), "Sostenibilidad democrática y cultura cívica: la cultura política de Nicaragua en cambio", Florisabel Rodriguez, Silvia Castro, and Rowland Espinoza. Costa Rica: Editorial Fundación UNA.
Orozco, Manuel, Rodolfo de la Garza, and Miguel Baraona. (1997), "El Impacto de las Remesas Familiares Hacia América Latina", *Cuadernos de Ciencias Sociales* 98, no. 43-62.
Ortega, Zoilamerica. (1996), *Desmovilizados de guerra en la construcción de la paz en Nicaragua*. Managua: Centro de Estudios Internacionales.
Padilla, David, and Elizabeth Houppert. (1993), "International Election Observing: Enhancing the Principle of Free and Fair Elections", *Emory International Law Review* 7: 73-132.
Padilla, Luis Alberto. (1995), "The United Nations and Conflict Resolution in Central America Peace Making and Peace Building in Internal Armed Conflict", *Estudios Internacionales* 6, no. 12 July.
Palmer, David Scott. (1996), "Peru: Collectivelly Defending Democracy", *Beyond*

Sovereignty: Collectively Defending Democracy in the Americas, Tom Farer. Baltimore: The Johns Hopkins University Press.

Parry, Geraint. (1992), "The Interweaving of Foreign and Domestic Policy Making", *Government and Opposition* 28, no. 2: 143-151.

Pastor, Robert A. (1987), *Condemned to Repetition: the United States and Nicaragua*. Princeton: Princeton University Press.

___. (1992), *Whirlpool: U.S. Foreign Policy toward Latin America and the Caribbean*, New Jersey: Princeton.

Petras, James, and Morris Morley. (1990), *US Hegemony under siege: class, politics and development in Latin America*. New York: Verso.

Pillar, Paul. (1983), *Negotiating Peace: War Termination as a Bargaining Process*. Princeton: Princeton University Press.

Powell, Charles. (1996), "International Aspects of Democratization: The Case of Spain", *The International Dimensions of Democratization*, Lawrence Whitehead. Oxford: Oxford University Press.

Przeworski, Adam, Michael Alvarez, Jose ANtonio Cheibub, and Fernando Limongi. (1996), "What Makes Democracies Endure?" *Journal of Democracy* 7, no. 1: 50-51.

Quigley, Kevin. (1997), *For democracy's sake : foundations and democracy assistance in Central Europe*. Washington, D.C., : Woodrow Wilson Center Press ; B (Distributed by John Hopkins University Press).

Raymond, Gregory A. (1997), "Problems and Prospects in the Study of International Norms", *Mershon International Studies Review* 41, no. 2 November: 205-246.

Richardson, Neil R. (1978), *Foreign Policy and Economic Dependence*. Austin: University of Texas Press.

Robinson, William I. (1992), *A Faustian Bargain: U.S. Intervention in the Nicaraguan Elections and American Foreign Policy in the Post-Cold War World*. Boulder: Westview Press.

Robinson, William I. (1996), *Promoting Polyarchy: Globalization, US Intervention and Hegemony*. Cambridge: Cambridge University Press.

Rojas Aravena, Francisco. (1990), *Costa Rica y el sistema internacional*. San Jose: FLACSO.

___. (1988), *Subditos o aliados, la politica exterior de Estados Unidos y Centro America*. San Jose: FLACSO.

Rosenau, James. (1997), *Along the Domestic-Foreign Frontier: Exploring Governance in a Turbulence World*, Cambridge: Cambridge University Press.

___. (1990), *Turbulence in World Politics*. London: Harvester.

Rouquie, Alain. (1994), *Guerras y Paz en América Central*, México: FCE.

Ruggie, John Gerard. (1998), *Constructing the World Polity*. New York: Routledge.

Russell, Gary. (1997), interview by author, Tape recording, Managua, Nicaragua, July-August.

Sakamoto, Yoshikazu. (1997), "Civil Society and democratic world order", in *Innovation and Transformation in International Studies*, Stephen Gill and

James H. Mittelman. Cambridge: Cambridge University Press.
Saldomado, Angel. (1996), *Nicaragua con el futuro en juego*. Managua: CRIES.
Sartori, Giovanni. (1994), *Exporting/Importing Democracy*. paper delivered for international conference held in Seoul, Korea.
Sassen, Saskia. (1996), *Losing Control? Sovereignty in an Age of Globalization*. New York: Columbia University Press.
Schirmer, Jennifer G. (1993), "Those who die for life cannot be called dead" Women and Human Rights Protest in Latin America, in Surviving Beyond Fear: Women, Children and Human Rights in Latin America, edited by Marjorie Agosin, New York: White Pine Press.
Schmitter, Philippe C. (1996), "The Influence of the International Context upon the Choice of National Institutions and Policies of Neo-Democracies", *The International Dimensions of Democratization*, Lawrence Whitehead. Oxford: Oxford University Press.
Schoultz, Lars. (1981), *Human Rights and United States Policy toward Latin America*. Princeton: Princeton University Press.
___. (1987), *National Security and United States Policy toward Latin America*. Princeton: Princeton University Press.
Schulz, Donald and Deborah Sundloff Schulz. (1994), *The United States, Honduras, and the Crisis in Central America*. Boulder: Westview Press.
Scott, David Clark. (1993), "U.S. Human Rights Group Criticizes Mexico's Military", *Christian Science Monitor*, 17 September: 6.
Scott, James M. (1996), *Deciding to Intervene*. Durham: Duke University Press.
Searle, John R. (1995), *The Construction of Social Reality*. New York: The Free Press.
SEC. (1996), *Condensado General de Observadores Internacionales*. Managua (internal document): Consejo Supremo Electoral (Comision de Observacion Electoral), November.
Seligson, Mitchell A. and John A. Booth. (1995), *Elections and Democracy in Central America*. Chapel Hill: The University of North Carolina Press.
Shain, Yossi. (1995), "Ethnic Diasporas and U.S. Foreign Policy", *Political Studies Quarterly* 109, no. 5
Sheffer, Gabriel. (1993), "Ethnic Diasporas: A Threat to Their Hosts?" *International Migration and Security*, Myron Weiner. Boulder: Westview Press.
SIDA. (1996), *Resume of Swedish Development Cooperation with Nicaragua*. Managua: Swedish Embassy, December.
SIDA. (1999) *Sida's Key Areas*. Stockholm, Sweden: Swedish International Development Agency, http://www.sida.se/.
Sikkink, Kathryn. (1996), "The Emergence, Evolution, and Effectiveness of the Latin American Human Rights Network", *Constructing Democracy: human rights, citizenship and society in Latin America*, Elizabeth and Eric Hershberg Jelin. Boulder: Westview Press.
___. (1993), "Human rights, principled issue-networks, and sovereignty in Latin America", *International Organization* 47, no. 3: 441- 441.
Sivard, Ruth Leger. (1995), *World military and social expenditures*, Leesburg, Va.:

WMSE Publications.
Smith, David. (1992), "Panama: Political parties, social crisis and democracy in the 1990s", *Political Parties and Democracy in Central America*, 213-236. William Leogrande Louis W. Goodman, and Johanna Mendelson Forman. Boulder: Westview Press.
Smith, Hazel. (1995), *European Union Foreign Policy and Central America*, London: St. Martin's Press.
Smith, Jackie, and Ron Pagnuco with George Lopez. (1998), "Globalizing Human Rights: The Work of Transnational Human Rights NGOs in the 1990s", *Human Rights Quarterly* 20: 379-412.
Smith, Tony. (1986), "The Underdevelopment of the Development Literature", ed. Atul Kohli. Princeton: Princeton University Press.
Smock, David and Chester Crocker. (1995), *African Conflict Resolution: The U.S. role in Peacemaking*. Washington, DC: US Institute of Peace.
Sojo, Carlos. (1991), *Costa Rica: política exterior y sandinismo*. San José: FLACSO.
___. (1991), "La Política del aliado inteligente: Costa Rica y Estados Unidos 1988-1989", in *Centroamérica: de Reagan a Bush*, Gabriel Aguilera, Abelardo Morales, and Carlos Sojo. San Jose: FLACSO.
Sorensen, Georg. (1998), *Democracy and democratization : processes and prospects in a changing world*, Boulder, Colorado: Westview Press.
Spalding, Rose J. (1994), *Capitalists and Revolution in Nicaragua: Opposition and Accomodation, 1979-1993*, Chapel Hill, North Carolina: The University of North Carolina Press.
Sparks, Allister. (1990), *The Mind of South Africa*. New York: Alfred A. Knopf.
Spence, Jack and George Vickers. (1994), *A negotiated revolution? A two year progress report on the Salvadoran peace accords*. Cambridge: Hemisphere Initiatives, March.
Stahler-Sholk, Richard. (1998), "External State Actors in the Central American Transitions", paper presented at the LASA conference.
Steiner, Henry. (1996), "Political Participation as a Human Right", in *International Human Rights in Context: law, politics, morals*, Henry J. Steiner, and Philip Alston. Oxford: Oxford University Press.
Steiner, Henry J., and Philip Alston. (1996), *International Human Rights in Context: law, politics, morals*. Oxford: Oxford University Press.
Taboada Teran, Alvaro. (1994), *Nicaragua: el crepusculo de la Vanguardia, horizontes internos e internacionales*. Managua: Fondo Editorial, Banco Central de Nicaragua.
Tinoco, Victor Hugo. (1989), *Conflicto y paz : el proceso negociador centroamericano*. Mexico: Editorial Mestiza.
Torres-Rivas, Edelberto. (1992), *El tamaño de nuestra democracia*. San Salvador: FLACSO.
___. (1996), "El Caos Democrático", *Nueva Sociedad* 144: 152-168.
Touraine, Alain. (1997), "What is Democracy?" Boulder: Westview Press.
Tsingos, Basilios. (1996), "Underwriting Democracy: The European Community and Greece", *The International Dimensions of Democratization*, Lawrence

Whitehead. Oxford: Oxford University Press.
Turner, Scott. (1998), "Global civil society, anarchy and governance: assesing an emerging paradigm", *Journal of Peace Research* 35, no. 1: 25-44.
UIA. (1998), *International organizations by year and by type 1909-1996*. Brussels, Belgium: Union of International Associations, http://www.uia.org/uiastats/stybv296.htm>(02-02-1999) 26 June.
UN. (2001), *Member State's Requests for Electoral Assistance to the United Nations System (since 1989 as of August 1999)*. New York: UN Electoral Assistance Division, Dept. of Political Affairs,
<http: //www.un.org/Depts/dpa/docs/website9.htm>.
UN Secretary General. (1996), *An Agenda for Democratization*, New York: UN General Assembly <http://www.un.org/.
____. (1997), *Enhancing the Effectiveness of the Principle of Periodic and Genuine Elections*, <http://www.un.org/Depts/dpa/docs/ Report97.htm> (11-01-1998): UN General Assembly, A/52/474, 16 October.
____. (1996), *Enhancing the Effectiveness of the Principle of Periodic and Genuine Elections*, <http://www.un.org/Depts/dpa/docs/ Report91.htm> (11-01-1998): UN General Assembly, November.
____. (1990), *Fifth Report by the U.N. Observer Mission to Verify the Electoral Process in Nicaragua*, New York: UN General Assembly, A/44/927.
____. (1993), *The situation in Central America: procedures for the establishment of a firm and lasting peace*. New York: UN General Assembly, A/47/912; A/46/955; A/49/585.
USAID. (1998), *Democracy*. Washington, DC: USAID, <http://www.info.usaid.gov/democracy/> (01-11-1998).
____. (1997), *Reuniones de ONG's con USAID: Fortalecimiento de la Sociedad Civil*. internal AID document: USAID Managua.
Vale, Peter. (1991), "Using every available weapon? International pressure and change in South Africa", *International Affairs Bulletin* 15, no. 2: 53-66.
Van Evera, Stephen. (1997), *Guide to Methods for Students of Political Science*. Ithaca, New York: Cornell University Press.
Vanderlaan, Mary B. (1986), *Revolution and Foreign Policy in Nicaragua*. Boulder: Westview Press.
Vargas, Oscar Rene. (1991), *Adonde va Nicaragua: perspectivas de una revolucion latinoamericana*. Managua: Ediciones Nicarao.
____, ed. (1996), *Nicaragua: gobernabilidad democrática y reconversión militar*, Managua: CEEN.
Vergara Meneses, Raul. (1987), *Centro America: la guerra de baja intensidad*. San Jose: CRIES-DEI.
Vilas, Carlos M. (1995), *Between Earthquakes and Volcanoes: Market, State and the Revolutions in Central America*, New York: Monthly Review Press.
____. (1984), *Perfiles de la Revolución Sandinista*, Havana: Casa de las Americas.
Waltz, Kenneth. (1979), *Theory of International Politics*. New York: McGraw Hills.
Waltz, Susan E. (1995), *Human Rights and Reform: changing the face of North African politics*. Berkeley: University of California Press.

Wapner, Paul and Lester Edwin J. Ruiz, (2000), *Principled World Politics: The Challenging Normative International Relations*. New York: Rowman & Littlefield Publishers.
Wehr, Paul and John Paul Lederach. (1991), "Mediating conflict in Central America", *Journal of Peace Research* 28, no. 1: pp. 85-98.
Whitehead, Lawrence. (1987), "International Aspects of Democracy", *Transitions from Authoritarian Rule: comparative perspectives*, Guillermo O'Donnell, Phillippe C. Schmitter, and Lawrence Whitehead. Oxford: Oxford University Press.
___. (1996), *The International Dimensions of Democratization*. Oxford: Oxford University Press.
Wiarda, Howard J. (1987), *The communist challenge in the Caribbean and Central America*. . Washington, D.C. : American Enterprise Institute for Public Policy Research.
___. (1997), *Cracks in the Consensus: Debating the Democracy Agenda in U.S. Foreign Policy*. Westport, Connecticut: Praeger.
Wippman, David. (1997), "Defending Democracy Through Foreign Intervention", *Houston Journal of International Law* 19: 659-687.
WOLA. (1990), *El Salvador: Is Peace Possible*. Washington.
Wola. (1989), *Establishing the Ground Rules: A Report on the Nicaraguan Electoral Process*. Washington DC: WOLA, August .
___. (1989), *Nicaragua: Election Monitor "National Reconciliation and Elections"*. Washington DC: WOLA, 4 August.
WOLA. (1989), *Nicaragua: Election Monitor, No. 2*. Washington DC: WOLA, September.
___. (1989), *Nicaragua: Election Monitor, No. 3*. Washington DC: WOLA, October.
___. (1989), *Nicaragua: Election Monitor, No. 4*. Washington DC: WOLA, November.
WOLA. (1991), *Nicaragua: Reconciliation Awaiting Recovery*. Washington DC: WOLA, April.
___. (1992), *Nicaragua Issue Brief #1*. Washington DC: WOLA, September.
___. (1992), *Nicaragua Issue Brief #2*. Washington DC: WOLA, December.
Zartman, William I. (1985), *Ripe for Resolution: conflict and intervention in Africa*. New York: Oxford University Press.
Zartman, I. William. (November 1991), "Conflict and resolution: contest, cost, and change ", *Annals of the American Academy of Political and Social Science* 518.
___. *Negotiating Internal conflicts*. (1993), Columbia: University of South Carolina Press.
___. *Elusive Peace: negotiating an end to civil wars*. (1995), Washington, D.C.: The Brookings Institution.
Zartman, William I. and J. Lewis Rasmussen. (1997), *Peacemaking in International Conflicts: methods and techniques*. Washington DC: US Institute of Peace.
Zuniga, Rene Herrera. (1994), *Nicaragua, el derrumbe negociado*. México: El Colegio de México.

Index

Alemán, Arnoldo, 97, 113, 114, 115, 116, 117, 118, 119, 120, 121
Arias, Oscar, 1, 46, 56, 66, 69, 73, 74, 75, 76, 83, 89, 104, 129
Carothers, Thomas, 18, 50, 82, 130
Carter Center, 46, 61, 62, 86, 98, 104, 130
CCPR, 38, 39, 40
Chamorro, Violeta, 2, 80, 84, 89, 90, 92, 93, 94, 95, 97, 99, 100, 101, 103, 104, 105, 106, 121, 131, 132
Conditionality, 25, 105
Consent, 22, 28, 105, 138
Contadora group, 55, 68, 74, 75, 76
Contras, 71, 79, 80, 92, 94
Costa Rica, 1, 2, 9, 56, 66, 69, 71, 72, 74, 75, 77, 79, 81, 104, 140, 141, 143
Democracy
    Definition of, 4
    Global spread, 7
    International pressures, 18
    International support to new democracies, 20
Democratic Charter, 49
Diamond, Larry, 4, 8, 15, 27, 29, 106, 132
Etica y Transparencia, 98, 122
European Union, 47, 48, 58, 98, 104, 122, 125, 143
Foreign aid, 55, 70, 105
Franck, 36, 37, 39, 133
FSLN, 66, 67, 72, 83, 84, 85, 88, 90, 92, 97, 98, 99, 113, 114, 115, 116, 117, 118, 119, 121, 122
Giddens, Anthony, 123, 134
Globalization and Sovereingty, 127
Held, David, 30, 32, 57, 123, 124, 125, 129, 135
IDEA, 46, 57, 58, 60, 61, 96, 129, 135
IFES, 46, 61
International actors
    Civil society movements, 12
    International Organizations, 12
    States, 9
International community, 1

Klotz, Audie, 17, 30, 31, 33, 36, 137
Latin America, 7, 13, 15, 20, 23, 41, 43, 48, 53, 68, 69, 70, 73, 74, 79, 89, 121, 130, 131, 132, 134, 135, 136, 138, 139, 140, 141, 142, 143
Liberal Alliance, 97
NDI, 62, 83, 84, 94, 98, 104, 107, 139
Nicaragua
    1979-1989, 56
    1990 elections, 90
    1990s, 57
    1996 elections, 99
    2001 election, 118
    Assistance for Democracy, 58
    Civil Society, 97
    Democratic transition, 102
    Peace negotiations, 80
    pre-1979, 53
Norms
    Advocacy for democracy, 49
    as theory in international relations, 33
    definition, 31
    Global conferences for democracy, 51
    Institutions, 40
    Sources of international norms, 35
    Support of democracy, 37
OAS, 1, 14, 15, 26, 27, 44, 48, 49, 56, 61, 66, 74, 76, 78, 79, 81, 86, 88, 89, 90, 98, 104, 105, 107, 108, 122, 130, 140
Ortega, Daniel, 82, 84, 86, 88, 89, 90, 92, 94, 95, 97, 98, 100, 106, 113, 115, 119, 120, 129, 136, 137, 141
PLC, 115, 116, 117, 118, 119, 121
Reagan, Ronald, 16, 53, 67, 68, 71, 72, 73, 82, 105, 110, 128, 129, 130, 136, 137, 138, 143
Rosenau, 1, 12, 30, 46, 81, 124, 142
Ruggie, John Gerard, 12, 31, 32, 137, 142
Sandinista National Liberation Front, 66, *See* FSLN
Schmitter, Philippe, 22, 25, 27, 140, 142, 145
Searle, John, 2, 31, 142